About the Author's

Author Abdul Olugbala Shakur served 32½ years in solitary confinement and author Joka Heshima Jinsai served 20 years in solitary confinement. While the two men endured inhumane brutalities throughout these decades, in a place meant to break their minds, spirits, and connections to family and the outside world, they found their freedom through the very mechanisms their keepers sought to destroy – the power of their words.

Black Panther Party Press Publishing

CONCRETE SCHOLARS

Volume I

Joka Heshima Jinsai
Abdul Olugbala Shakur

Concrete Scholars Selected Writings: Volume I

ISBN: 9798653937064

Book cover and interior design: Quaitie Siverly
Editors: Quaitie Siverly and John Reimer

Printed in the United States of America
Published by Black Panther Press Publishing

We dedicate this book to the following New Afrikan Freedom Fighters

Bunchy Carter	Saani Al-Azeez
George Jackson	Twyman Meyers
W.L. Nolen	Melvin Rema Kerney
Assata Shakur	Alfred Kambui Butler
Nehanda Abiodun	Woodie Changa Green
Afeni Shakur	Sandra Pratt
Chokwe Lumumba	Dessie Woods
Nubia Lumumba	Cheryl Todd
Safiya Bukhari	Nuh Washington
Mtyari Shabaka Sundiata	Jalil Muntaqim
Zayd Shakur	Herman Bell
William Christmas	John Savage
Jonathon Jackson	Sylvester Bell
Jeffry Khatari Gualden	Bobby Hutton
Fred Hampton	Cleveland Edwards
John Andaliwa Clark	Alvin Jug Miller
Dr. Mutulu Shakur	Sekou Odinga
Fati Yero Kambon	Abdul Majid
Adama Kambon	Bashir Hameed
Howard Tole	Masai Mugmuk
Sundiata Acoli	Maliki Shakur Latine
Kuasi Balagoon	Kojo Bomani Sababu
Atiba Shana	Dhoruba Bin-Wahad
Muhammad Ahmad	Ifoma Modibo Kambon
Lumumba Shakur	Ashanti Alston
Tupac Amaru Shakur	Fulani Sunni-Ali
James McClain	Bilal Sunni-Ali
Russel Maroon Shoats	Sharifa Shakur
Rukia Chokwe	Jihad Abdulmumit

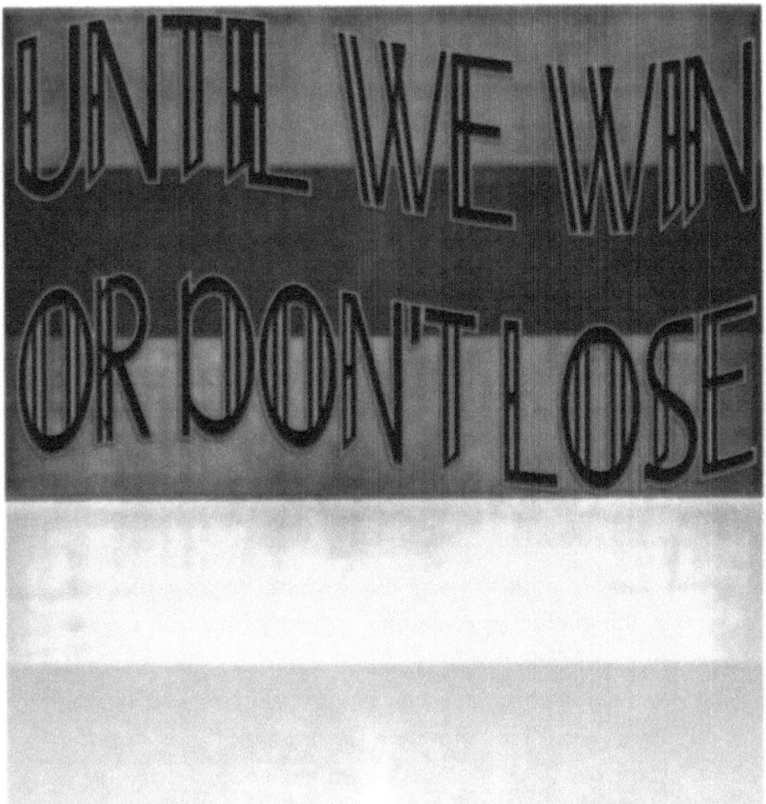
UNTIL WE WIN
OR DON'T LOSE

Acknowledgments

Our thanks to the many Komrades, activists and professionals who contributed their insight, support and expertise to make this work possible, including all those whose political thoughts and actions contributed to our own development.

We give special thanks to Mary and Willie Ratcliff of the *San Francisco Bay View National Black Newspaper* for their years of support and for providing so many imprisoned political activists a platform to share our ideas with the world.

We would like to thank our dear friend and comrade Annabelle Parker for her years of support, activism, printing, editing and online promotion of our work and that of many of our Komrades.

Our thanks to John Reimer for his exceptional line editing work on this manuscript.

We express our deep heartfelt thanks and appreciation to Quaitie Siverly for her tireless work to bring this manuscript to publishing. Her hours of reading, editing, re-editing, collaborating with us, and resource expenditure made this book possible. Thanks Sis.

Finally, we would like to thank our Families for their unwavering love and support over these many years of struggle: Abdul's wife, Sharifa Shakur, his daughter Akilah Muhammad and his niece Dani Muhammad, along with Joka Heshima Jinsai's wife Sheron Greenfield-Denham, his sister Duvon Denham and his son Julian Ryan Burks-Denham.

We thank you all for your love and support.

                    – Abdul Olugbala Shakur
                    – Joka Heshima Jinsai

TABLE OF CONTENTS

Concrete Scholars Selected Writings: Volume I

4

JOKA HESHIMA JINSAI

Concrete Scholars, George Jackson University, GJU

Introduction

The laws of Dialectical Materialism/Materialist Dialectics dictate that in order to transform adverse social conditions, you must employ their *opposite*. The U.S. has long denounced nations like China, Iran, and the former Soviet Republics for subjecting political dissidents to summary imprisonment, solitary confinement, and other forms of torture, while simultaneously presiding over the single largest Domestic Torture program on Earth. This Domestic Torture program carried out in Amerikkka's supermax style solitary confinement units, often referred to as "SHU's" (Security Housing Units) across state and federal prisons is the most comprehensive example of mass psychological and physical torture in post WWII times. The function of such units, as stated by former Marion warden Ralph Aron is, "to control Revolutionary attitudes in the prison systems and society at large."[1]

How they achieve this end is through a combination of Scheinerian operant conditioning, learned helplessness, sensory deprivation, indefinite solitary confinement, constant illumination; in short, torture. We quickly found that social control was not the primary function of the SHU torture unit – instead, its focus was directed towards breaking men's minds in hopes of eliciting information and/or coercing them into becoming informants or active agents of the state. The political nature of its motive force, primarily where New Afrikans are concerned, was clear from the outset. The only segments of the New Afrikan prisoner population targeted for indefinite solitary confinement in the SHU were those who – through expression or action – demonstrated that their ideology was New Afrikan Revolutionary Nationalism/Revolutionary Scientific Socialism. Those who owned books and literature about Black History espoused culturally conscious ideas or resisted blatant abuses were labeled "gang members," and consigned to the bowels of these torture units for decades. There, prison administrators made it clear; the only way we would ever leave these tombs is to "parole, debrief or die."

The United Nations Convention Against Torture and Other Cruel, Inhuman and Degrading Treatment and Punishment defines torture as:

> ...any act by which severe pain or suffering, whether physical or mental, is intentionally inflicted on a person for such purposes as obtaining from him (or her) or a third person information or a confession, punishing him (or her) for an act he or a third person has committed or is suspected of having committed, or intimidating or coercing him (or her) or a third person, or for any reason based on discrimination of any kind, when such pain or suffering is inflicted by or at the instigation of or with the consent or acquiescence of a public official or other person acting in an official capacity.[2]

The behavior modification techniques employed by the state did break the minds of many men, but just as the cold breeds ice, this repression bread resistance. The very class of Prisoners most severely targeted for political repression, was the same class of Prisoners most determined to end it: the New Afrikan Revolutionary Nationalist.

As diabolical as the state's political repression became against us, the more imaginative and determined we became to not only overcome the abuses we were subjected to, but to correct the ills of society at the heart of our National oppression. It was in the heart of this ever evolving struggle where Abdul Olugbala Shakur and I gave birth to the concept of *Concrete Scholars*.

This collection of essays and articles, culled from our works published in the *San Francisco Bay View National Black Newspaper,* is an unvarnished view of that struggle; a scathing indictment of the contradictions inherent in the U.S. racist/capitalist arrangement, and the efforts of those with the least interest in its perpetuation to transform the nature and structure of this society.

What you will read in these pages, the analysis, deliberation and activism, is our effort to make this world a freer, more just, and equal place for us all. It is *all we do,* all day every day in this cell. It is our determination that our results are directly proportional to our efforts, and it is our hope, as you read these words, that internal Revolution blooms in you, invoking a new perspective on social life, and an obligation to join us in this struggle for a new and brighter world.

Until we win or don't lose.

CHAPTER

ONE

ABDUL OLUGBALA SHAKUR

ononoonononoonoonoono

What is Solitary Confinement?

9

ABDUL OLUGBALA SHAKUR

What is Solitary Confinement?

At first glance, and from its most simplistic perspective, the question, "What is solitary confinement?" appears to be rhetorical, if not insulting, but you would be surprised, if not incredulous, how many prison rights activists are at a loss when I pose the question to them. Even more perplexing, many prisoners are only able to provide the standard but antiquated response, which is: a prisoner in a cell behind a solid door, in which he/she is isolated from other prisoners and human contact.

By no means am I implying this is the incorrect answer. What I am implying, however is; right answer, but wrong century!

From the beginning of the 20th century on, and further back, this answer was applicable, but at the end of the 20th century and into the start of the 21st century, its theoretical concept remained, but its tactical application has transformed, directly due to two primary factors: 1) advancement in technology and 2) a deeper and more functional knowledge of the process as a direct result of analyzing past applications of solitary confinement and its desired ramifications.

Yes, isolation is still the quintessential criterion that helps to identify and define what solitary confinement is, but in the 21st century, the answer is more complicated than just saying "isolated from all other prisoners." The government and the Prison Industrial Slave Complex (PISC) love holding onto the old definition, where physical isolation is the only criterion for defining what solitary confinement is, knowing the science of solitary confinement isolation has expanded beyond its original applications.

I use Alcatraz Prison to both qualify and quantify our analysis, as it pertains to the tactical evolutionary development of solitary confinement. No one can question or doubt that Alcatraz was the epitome of solitary confinement and isolation, but Alcatraz equally represented the new face of solitary confinement. Each unit consisted of multiple tiers, with at least 20 prisoners on each tier; they even went to the exercise yard together.

All these factors contradict the standard definition of solitary confinement; the isolation of a single individual prisoner was no longer a qualifying criterion to define what solitary confinement was. The Prison Industrial Slave Complex in its modern state has been able to achieve isolation, even where there are multiple prisoners located in a single unit or pod.

Alcatraz Prison illustrated an evolutionary development in the tactical application of solitary confinement or isolation. It dispels the notion that solitary confinement only applies to a prisoner who is isolated from all other prisoners.

Marion Federal Prison is another example; no one has ever questioned that Marion isolation units did not meet the criteria for solitary confinement. When these particular units were opened, the federal government boasted of its isolation and specifically referred to it as solitary confinement. Yet these same units consisted of a row of multiple cells, where prisoners could communicate and see each other and, at one time, prison officials had placed TVs on the tiers for the prisoners to watch.

The federal prison at Florence is another example; each cell is issued a TV, and communication with other prisoners is open. But you will never hear the government or the Bureau of Prisons (BOP) say Florence federal prisoners are not in solitary confinement.

San Quentin State Prison Adjustment Center, between 1968 and 1986, or Soledad Prison's O Wing between 1969 and 1979 are examples to substantiate CDCr's transformative tactical applications of solitary confinement.

The CDCr and the state government are using the same characteristics I have identified in these other prisons to attempt to debunk the allegations that prisoners in Pelican Bay State Prison (PBSP) are being held in solitary confinement isolation. During each of our hunger strikes, we heard representatives from both the state government and the CDCr try to refute the allegations that prisoners are being held in solitary confinement at PBSP.

Their basic argument consisted of: 1) Prisoners being held in the security housing unit (SHU) at PBSP are allowed to purchase and possess TVs; 2) Some of them are allowed cellmates; and 3) The eight prisoners in a pod can communicate with each other. The three primary points in their argument are elements you could find at Alcatraz when it was open, or Marion Federal Prison when it was considered the most secure prison in the U.S., and now Florence Federal Prison. No one questions whether prisoners in these prisons are held in solitary confinement.

People, this is why it is imperative for us to articulate in a comprehensive way the transforming tactical applications of solitary confinement. So retrospection is a prerequisite towards navigating the people through the evolutionary development and stages of solitary confinement.

Alcatraz, Marion and Florence all represent a stage of development in the tactical and strategic evolution in the application of solitary confinement. But PBSP epitomizes that evolution — tactically, strategically, technically and scientifically. Pelican Bay State Prison redefined what solitary confinement is in America and how it can be applied even in an environment where there are multiple prisoners with TVs.

PBSP has taken isolation to a scientific level; it has become so sophisticated in its execution it is barely detected on the average prison rights activist radar. In fact, the average prisoner is often blind to the deliberate manipulation of the conditions now required to compliment the implementation of the new application of solitary confinement.

It is true isolation is key to solitary confinement, and one cannot exist without the other, but what PBSP has mastered is the orchestrated conditions which identify and exploit the multiplicity of the tactical mechanics of isolation. Physical isolation is just one form of isolation, but if you were to dissect the anatomy of isolation, you will then discover its multiplicity, such as: 1) social isolation; 2) racial and cultural isolation; 3) ideological and political isolation; 4) religious and spiritual isolation and 5) geographical isolation.

Allow me to employ a civilian example to illustrate the utilization of the multiplicity of isolation, before I briefly elaborate on its utility within PBSP SHU. Let's say I have an eight bedroom house, and each room has a TV. I pick eight people to live in this house. There are four rooms upstairs and four rooms downstairs. I select the following four people to live in the upstairs rooms: 1) a Jewish Holocaust survivor, 2) a Nazi concentration camp guard, 3) a member of Hamas and 4) an Israeli soldier.

And downstairs I select the following four people: l) Nat Turner, 2) a slave master who enslaved Brother Nat Turner's family, 3) a liberal and 4) Rush Limbaugh.

I deliberately identified all contradictory bodies of politics; can you imagine the outcome of such an orchestrated dynamic? Even though there are no bars on the bedroom doors, I have orchestrated conditions designed to facilitate isolation. Most of these individuals would avoid each other and stay to themselves; I have manipulated conditions that produced a solitary state.

Though there are eight people in this house, there will be little to no communication. For the most part, they will stay to themselves, reinforcing conditions for isolation or solitary confinement; but it was I who orchestrated these conditions, knowing the inevitable outcome.

These individuals will become isolated in a solitary state compelled by the conditions orchestrated by me.

Now, let's replace the eight rooms with eight cells in a pod with the same racial, cultural, geographic, political, religious and socially diverse contradictions, but intensified tenfold. This is the new anatomy of solitary confinement isolation.

People, please understand, the new architectural structure of today's prisons cannot accommodate the old forms of solitary confinement or isolation – or even torture. Their infrastructural designs have given birth to new forms of solitary confinement or isolation, as well as torture, thus redefining what solitary confinement is in the 21st century. The modern-day dungeons are more technically sophisticated, intricate and illusory to the average person in society.

I would be amiss not to use this medium to elaborate and expose the malevolent and nefarious parasitic nature of the CDCr's methods for executing social isolation. Social isolation has a dual nature or function: 1) to facilitate the isolation process as it pertains to precision targeting of a specific prisoner, and 2) to serve as a tactical instrument in the service of the prison's torture program.

As have stated above, it is obligatory for me to use this medium to expose the tactics which are being used to implement social isolation as it relates to precision targeting for the sole purpose of increasing the degree of isolation for a specific target – i.e. a prisoner. These tactics are criminal and in violation of our allegedly constitutionally protected rights, and the CDCr agents of repression, such as the Office of Correctional Safety (OCS), Institutional Gang Investigations Unit (IGI) and the Investigative Services Unit (ISU), develop and deploy these criminal tactics with impunity – and I have been their primary target for extreme social isolation.

Social isolation has both an internal and external component. The internal component basically consists of placing a prisoner in a pod or unit with other prisoners who are openly ideologically, geographically, socially or racially hostile to that particular prisoner. This ensures he/she will not communicate and/or confide in other prisoners in his/her pod, thus isolating their target.

However, to complete this isolation, the CDCr agents of repression must execute the external component of social isolation, which simply means, destroy and/or sabotage the targeted prisoner's primary outside support or contact. I will use my personal experience to illustrate the external component of the tactical application of social isolation.

My wife, Gwendolyn James (Sharifa Shakur), my spiritual father, Dr. Donald R. Evans, and my spiritual brother and comrade, Rashid Ali, became the main targets for the agents of repression, and this was the diabolical scheme these pigs used to sabotage my connection with my loved ones. IGI and ISU had fraudulently accused my wife and my spiritual father and brother of being drop-boxes for the Black Guerrilla Family (BGF). A drop-box is an address that has been identified by authorities as a medium, where members from the same prison organization, or group, or gang, communicate with each other, which is prohibited.

These allegations were false, but nevertheless they were banned from corresponding with me, and I with them. These racist pigs destroyed my marriage and disconnected me from my spiritual father and brother.

During a 2005 evidentiary hearing, T.D. Hawkes, the head of TGI/ISU at the time, testified under oath there is no evidence to support the allegations that my wife and my spiritual father and brother were drop-boxes for the BGF. Even the judge in this matter, Judge W. Follett, in Marcus Harrison v. Pelican Bay State Prison, Case No. HCPB-04-5054, stated for the record, and I quote, "Well, the drop-box is a huge issue. If there was a drop-box, I think you would win hands down. There's no evidence. There's no evidence of a drop-box present."

But yet I was punished for these fraudulent allegations, along with my loved ones. Even after that decision, IGI and ISU continued to use those false allegations to justify the continued ban on my correspondence with my wife and my spiritual father and spiritual brother.

After 13 years of being disconnected, my spiritual father and I reconnected in 2013, but our reunion was filled with grief. He had informed me his spiritual son, my spiritual brother, whom these pigs had unjustly banned me from writing to, had passed away. He is now with the ancestors.

My spiritual father and I decided to resume our working relationship but, as anticipated, a new crew of IGI and ISU launched their illegal attacks with hope and intent of sabotaging our reunion. This time, they accused my spiritual father and me of being co-conspirators in an illicit organization. See http://nabsio.org/ for more information.

By the way, my spiritual father is 87 years old and has been a New Afrikan freedom fighter over 50 years, fearlessly serving our people and community, only to be criminalized by a bunch of racist, so-called law enforcers!

These recent attacks are documented, and I have shared the documentation with attorney Carol Strickman during a recent visit and have sent copies to Mary Ratcliff, editor of the Bay View newspaper. As you can see, there is no limit to what the agents of repression at CDCr will do to execute their task of isolating one of their primary targets – and everyone out there is fair game.

Before the death of my beloved mother in 2008, she became a target along with others, but the agents of repression, IGI and ISU, employed a different scheme. As most people know, I am a New Afrikan Revolutionary Nationalist (NARN) Muslim. I had been connected with my spiritual identity for over 30 years, but suddenly my spiritual name was considered fictitious. I was no longer allowed to use my spiritual name in my outgoing mail or address it on my envelopes for a two month period.

IGI and ISU confiscated approximately 20 outgoing letters, two of which were to my mother. When I received a card from my mother inquiring why she had not heard from me, it was her concern for me that compelled me to temporarily set aside my beliefs so I could write my mother. It was like the mini-series "Roots," when the slave master forced Kunta Kinte to proclaim his slave name: Toby! Instead of a whip, they used the pain they inflicted on my mother to compel me by proxy to proclaim my slave name: James Harvey.

However, by this time it was too late. I was later informed by my counsellor my mother had passed away, so she never had the opportunity to read my letter. Though I would eventually win an out-of-court settlement concerning this issue, it did not compensate for the pain these racist pigs caused me and my beloved mother!

People, the tactics IGI and ISU use to achieve social isolation are not only cruel, but criminal. Our families and loved ones are unjustly targeted and victimized by these racist, cowardly pigs in the name of 21st century solitary confinement!

People, the new form of solitary confinement is more precise in its execution. Its inherent flexibility, its pliable tactical application and precision targeting are evident within the daily functions of Pelican Bay State Prison.

Before I conclude this analysis, I would like to provide an additional example to illustrate the utility of the CDCr applications of socio-ideological isolation. As I previously stated, each pod has eight cells, four on the top and four on the bottom, but each individual cell in that pod is subjected to different degrees of isolation. Some are more isolated than others; this illustrates its precision.

When IGI and ISU first moved us to the Short Corridor, they had designated one cell per pod specifically for New Afrikan revolutionary prisoners. This was a conscious effort to isolate our New Afrikan revolutionary class – not just a physical isolation, but political, ideological, cultural, racial and social isolation as well.

Some of us are more isolated than others, making our solitary confinement more complete. But make no mistake about it; the security housing unit (SHU) represents the modern day solitary confinement!

Most people in society are perceptively trapped within an antiquated theoretical concept of what solitary confinement isolation is, while totally overlooking the fact that even Alcatraz for the most part did not meet the same criteria that characterizes solitary confinement. In fact, Alcatraz represented the dawning of a new theoretical concept, which was mass solitary confinement isolation.

Alcatraz was a clear prognosticator of what was to come, i.e. the maxi-max control unit prisons!

So, back to the question: What is solitary confinement? It is no longer a simple question with a simple answer, and the PISC is fully aware of this, because they know for the most part the vast majority of the people in society have an antiquated picture of what solitary confinement isolation is.

The public doesn't realize that under the new architectural structure of the maxi-max control unit prisons, the theoretical concept of solitary confinement has evolved. And it is incumbent upon us as activists, both inside and outside the walls, to re-educate the masses!

People, by no means is this a complete analysis and/or description of solitary confinement isolation, but I believe it is the first analysis that speaks to the evolutionary development and multiplicity of solitary confinement. If you have any questions concerning this analysis, feel free to reach me:

Abdul Olugbala Shakur, C48884

James Harvey

B-2-128

P. O. Box 5102,

Delano, CA 93216,

Kern Valley State Prison

.

CHAPTER

TWO

ABDUL OLUGBALA SHAKUR

The Vortex of Dementia

Though I have been active in the struggle for practically all my life, from a Panther cub to an urban guerrilla in the service of the underground, I have never considered myself to be a writer or at least not a good writer, but I felt it was imperative for me to conjure up whatever hidden skills I may possess to find the words to articulate this man-made construct that many of you out there call the prison industrial complex. For many of us trapped within its catacomb of solitary madness, this man-made construct of nefarious intent possesses a more sinister title: the vortex of dementia.

For the vast majority of us, when we initially entered these gates of hell, the protection of our physical being was of paramount concern, not realizing the booty bandits were the least of our worries. This realization doesn't become manifest in its fullness until we enter into its twisted, officially sanctioned vortex in the Security Housing Unit, or SHU, where our inherent stability becomes subjected to conditions specifically designed with both deliberate and malicious intent to disfigure our basic grasp on our sanity. Often times these conditions are subtle, but very effective nonetheless.

My first three years in the Security Housing Unit (SHU) were a blur. Any attempt to probe my sanity was undetected by my conscious awareness. But it was my fourth year in isolation that my captor's motives revealed themselves. While in the Adjustment Center at San Quentin State Prison, I was arbitrarily placed in the "quiet cell" – no running water, no lights, no mattress or blankets, just my boxer shorts and T-shirt.

I didn't sleep at all that first night; I was still trying to wrap my sensibility around my new reality. The cell had the stench of urine and fecal matter and on each side of my cell there were screams of torment and constant banging on my walls, obviously an attempt orchestrated by my captors to deprive me of sleep while I contemplated the now visible probes into my sanity.

Many of you who are unaware of the overall objective of the prison industrial slave-complex may be quick to dismiss the above experience as an aberration, not an elaborate scheme designed to break the spirit and torment the minds of its captives – the New Afrikan revolutionary prisoners in particular. On the 10th day of being in the quiet cell, my neighbors were informed that if they did not kick on my wall late at night, they'd not be removed from the quiet cell, a clear incentive for their complicity to facilitate my captors' endeavors to rob me of my sanity.

For an entire month my neighbors kicked on my walls, so losing myself in sleep to escape this psychological torture was not an option. I was forced to confront this deliberate assault on my sanity. This scheme would repeat itself two more times, each time longer than the next. The second time was approximately 45 days and the third time was 90 days.

Then I was emergency transferred to old Folsom in 1985. San Quentin State Prison had told the Folsom administration that I was involved in a conspiracy to murder staff, which was a blatant lie. I was not even in the unit where the guard was killed. But this lie was designed to evoke hostility and violence upon my arrival to Folsom.

Their plan worked. When I got to Folsom, I was placed in four-point restraints on a table butt naked. This went on for three days. I was then placed in the quiet cell in 4-A for an additional six months.

Then in 1987 I was placed in the first ever bedrock unit – I along with 24 white prisoners. I was the only New Afrikan (Black) prisoner assigned to this unit and spent approximately eight months in an environment designed to encourage a physical attack on me.

I was eventually released from Bedrock (i.e. Behavioral Control Unit) once my captors realized their plan didn't work. About four months later, I was placed back into Bedrock where I spent over a year. Both Corcoran and Pelican Bay State Prison were modeled after the Bedrock units. My second return to Bedrock was under the false allegation that I was involved in a conspiracy to assault prison staff. In response to this fabricated charge, I was physically assaulted and Tasers were placed on my testicles while I was handcuffed behind my back.

The above experiences represented the traditional methods of both psychological and physical torture, each challenging the resilience of my mental health, which I admit was beginning to succumb to the seduction of dementia.

Then in 1989, I entered the gladiator yards of Corcoran State Prison, where fights were staged daily for the pleasure of our sadistic captors. Though I received only two disciplinary reports, I was involved in at least 14 staged fights – another experience that took a toll on my already exhausted sanity.

This was (and is) a sanctioned assault of attrition being waged upon our mental health, a constant probing of our undiagnosed psychoses. Dementia was beginning to look more enticing, as I watched hundreds of prisoners around me surrender to the temptation of insanity, an escape from the harsh reality of sensory deprivation.

Many have asked how I survived 30½ years of solitary confinement isolation under constant assault on my mental state: I tell them, first of all, my ordeal is far from being over, so I have yet to survive my isolation, but I'm surviving in spite of my (our) situation.

For me, I believe identifying the symptoms is essential in resisting the attraction of dementia. Many convicts, because of the stigma attached to dementia, deny any symptoms. I don't care who you are – anybody who has spent 20 years or more in solitary such as the Security Housing Unit is going to have some symptoms. Though they may be subtle, they have the potential to mature into a full blown psychosis, if ignored. This is why I believe that embracing the symptoms helps us to subdue them. I recognized my symptoms 20 years ago and I refused to give into them, but it is a constant battle. Dementia is forever present, waiting to claim our sanity.

I entered the cold corridors of Pelican Bay State Prison that have exposed me to a new form of mental torture, a more subtle but sophisticated and systematic assault on one's senses, a deprivation so complete that it leaves one drowning within the depths of one's own emptiness. Before I close, I would like to briefly touch on a hypothesis that I've yet to hear anyone speak on, which I believe is worthy of further examination, and that is the Stockholm Syndrome. Many people became aware of this syndrome during the Patty Hearst trial, when she was witnessed on camera robbing a bank with her alleged captors. Simply put, the Stockholm Syndrome is when a captive begins to emulate the characteristics and/or belief system of his/her captor(s).

Many prisoners don't have a clue that they are emulating the same cowardly and immoral practices of their captors. I provide you with two brief examples:

1. First of all, the prison guard is an active participant within the CDCR-sanctioned torture scheme. Guards will identify a number of noises that they believe will serve to agitate and/or irritate prisoners. For example: loud whistling, slamming our food port, stomping up and down the stairs while we sleep, talking loud over the PA system, just to name a few. Once identified, staff

would begin to incorporate these torturous tactics in their daily routine.

But so-called convicts have also adopted these methods. I have witnessed a number of times so-called convicts direct our captor's scheme towards other convicts, thus collaborating with our captor's to wage psychological torture on their fellow convicts. As New Afrikan revolutionaries, we call these so-called convicts collaborators. I believe these so-called convicts are suffering from Stockholm Syndrome. I personally tell them about it every time I witness it, but for the most part to no avail. They are so far gone into the syndrome they have become captors (guards) by proxy.

2.   The Security Housing Unit (SHU) is a deliberate construct, and sensory deprivation is the product of a sick mind. Anyone who manages and profits from such a destructive scheme is void of any sense of humanity, especially when she/he can work in this environment and completely ignore the impact it is having on its captives.

You often become a product of your environment. If it's devoid of any sense of humanity and moral redemption, it is going to produce a product of like values. Many prisoners upon release are emulating the lack of humanity and redemption displayed daily by their captors; unfortunately, society suffers as a result via reoffending. That's a deliberate ploy designed to guarantee their return and the survival of the prison industrial slave-complex. I ask, what can you produce from a depraved environment? I believe recidivism has a mental component that is directly linked to our captors.

Being in prison alone has an impact on our mental state. But within the control unit prisons, there exists a deliberate and systematic assault on our sanity with a clear purpose. If state departments of corrections and the federal Bureau of Prisons can weaken our mental stability, we then become more vulnerable to the trappings of recidivism.

A disciplined mind allows us to resist any temptations that can bring us back to prison, such as drugs and alcohol or even negative friends. The key to resolving this matter lies with us as prisoners.

The prison system and the SHU is not going to shut down anytime soon. So we will have to be more realistic and pragmatic in our approach to addressing the mental health of prisoners. We can start off as prisoners by pledging we'll not become collaborators with the CDCR in their endeavor to assault our sanity!

ABDUL OLUGBALA SHAKUR

Sensory Deprivation: An Unnatural Death

The following assessment is far from being complete; it is a brief
analysis compelled by a question an activist posed to me: How
does sensory deprivation (S.D.) impact the psyche of those prisoners
who have been subjected to long-term solitary confinement? Actually,
this text is but a modified letter that I wrote in response to the above
question.

Most people in society are unfamiliar with the term "sensory
deprivation;" its terminology is not used within a daily societal
vernacular. And this is why: I believe it is imperative for us as
prisoners, who have endured the blunt forces of this deprivation, to
articulate its tortuous impositions upon our very humanity.

The intent is to dull our natural senses to touch, smell, taste,
sight and hearing, while simultaneously attempting to suffocate our
human spirit. It is a means of facilitating our unnatural death within
the catacomb of this concrete construct serving as our burial as they
introduce their step down pilot program which is equivalent to
scripting the obituary to the demise of our humanity.

Admittedly, this task to navigate through the vortex of dementia
that can be brought on by confinement to the Security Housing Unit,

or SHU, with the intent to convey its inherent peculiarities will be a toilsome and laborious assignment, though many may boast of its simplicity. But trust me, for those of us who have been held hostage within the confines of the CDCR SHU between 20 and 40 years, we are still struggling to wrap our consciousness around the scope and profundity of the ramifications of S.D. (sensory deprivation), for it is constantly revealing complex variables within its destructive capacity.

But in spite of its difficulties, it is an obligatory prerequisite that we forge a comprehensive blueprint designed to assist us in our endeavors to magnify for the outside world, the malignity of S.D., so we have become psychologically battered embedded reporters for the people, with the sincere hope of inviting you into our fight for justice and the restoration of humanity. Though this is not a complete assessment, I believe it would provide you with a glimpse into the ills of S.D. and that this would encourage other SHU survivors to present their assessment.

I realize many of you are becoming exasperated with my self-proclaimed inability to write and/or express myself, but each time I attempt to put pen to paper it becomes a struggle between my mind and the symptoms of a deprived psyche; I no longer have the capacity to concentrate. I tend to wander and become distracted by the most abstract and/or trivial thoughts.

So, for me, the act of writing in itself becomes a burdensome task, but yet I love to write, to propagate our revolutionary culture of resistance. I have disciplined my mind not to be distracted and I have developed a process that allows me to write in spurts while maintaining my focus on the task at hand.

A lack of concentration is no doubt a symptom of a sensory deprived mind that many of us who have spent decades in SHU have in common, a symptom that permeates all prison systems across the country, qualifying itself as a substantiated symptom.

Those with a disciplined mind can resist this symptom, but once you lose that ability, and surrender to the symptom of a loss of concentration, your mind will begin to wander uncontrollably until it finds comfort in the erratic chaos that lies beneath one's self-awareness, flirting with the seduction of insanity; as one probes deeper into its solace, away from the conscious reality where torment fornicates with the senses, challenging the equilibrium between the mind and the spirit.

People, escaping the harsh reality of solitary confinement, for some, may console their mind, a parallel space that takes one far away from this man-made hell. Though they are physically confined, their minds are in another space, between the conscious and subconscious – the equidistance where the cognitive dissonance theory defines the moment. We don't condemn them for succumbing to the temptation of escape; it is not their fault. They are the victims of an evil construct, a reminder for the rest of us the desired goal of S.D.

Some may even wonder why would I initiate this analytical assessment, implying that a lack of concentration is a principal symptom in prognosticating the initial effects of S.D. The disciplined mind is our first line of defense, and the architects of S.D. understood this. In order for S.D. to achieve its desired goals, it must penetrate our first line of defense, and once we lose that focus, we become more vulnerable to the seductive trappings of S.D. So the battle of demarcation occurs at the periphery of our conscious discernment of the particular, for it is here where our fate is determined, and the symptoms can rapidly precipitate into a psychosis that has the potential to hold our sanity hostage in perpetuity.

When the senses are so deprived, it petitions recompense that embodies a commiserated reciprocity that momentarily encapsulates our attention. There exist numerous examples to illustrate the validity of this observation. Prisoners, political prisoners and POWs who have spent time in isolation – solitary confinement – throughout the world have reported that while in isolation they often sought out interaction with the rodents and/or bugs that invade their torturous cubicles.

Instead of reviling them, they would invite the temporary distraction and begin to identify with the rat or bug. This is not a phenomenon that is only associated with prisoners in other countries; it is equally common among prisoners in the U.S. In Pelikkkan Bay State Prison (PBSP) many of us, since our arrival, have captured a frog or spider and kept it as a pet, something that most of us would have never done prior to our incarceration, a clear illustration to corroborate our findings that this behavior is a direct result of S.D.

For me it was more like a revelation. I recalled as a manchild I used to catch bugs and butterflies and place them in jars. I would poke holes in the lid. I would also place food in the jar, or what I thought was the food they ate. As a young manchild, I could never comprehend why my insects would try to escape. I had provided them with free room and board. But now I finally understand. Even though I have free room and board, I equally desire to escape my artificial home. Though our senses are deprived, we are constantly compensating, and it is in this process that we reconfirm our sanity.

Psychological torture in Amerikkka is real, not an illusion conjured up by disgruntled prisoners.

Sensory deprivation (S.D.) – make no mistake about it – is a tool of psychological torture, and our survival by no means repudiates its destructive capacity. It is not a tool that leaves obvious physical wounds. This is an art of torture that by design attacks the minds and spirits of its intended targets, attempting to incapacitate our sense of humanity, reducing us into a catatonic stupor or a chronic cycle of recidivism, addicted to the smell and touch of concrete and steel.

We have heard the warden, the overseer of this concrete plantation, on a number of occasions attempting to mitigate the severity of the SHU and S.D. He would often tell the media how we are allowed to purchase TVs in the SHU and unfortunately many people in society tend to accept the implications that a TV somehow compensates for the impact of solitary confinement and S.D. Even a prison rights activist asked me about the warden's statement.

I told her, if you were placed in the middle of Chernobyl, a nuclear and highly radioactive wasteland, and given a 42-inch flat screen TV with all the available channels of the world and all the free food you can eat, this doesn't abrogate the fact that you are trapped in the middle of a radioactive deathtrap that is designed to inflict pain upon your physical being and lead inevitability to an unnatural death.

People, the TV is not a privilege afforded by our overseer. To the contrary, it is a calculated injurious contrivance devised to impede our adroitness to develop the necessary defenses to empower us to resist the trappings of S.D. It is more of a detriment than an asset. Why do you think they have never removed TVs from the SHU? This is confirmation that the TV is, in fact, a tactical instrument in support of executing S.D. in its fullest arrangement. So please understand the facts: having a TV or radio in solitary confinement doesn't change the reality of our situation, which is the SHU is equivalent to solitary confinement and that S.D. is a form of psychological torture that can produce physical pain.

Though we are SHU survivors, we are not immune to the impact of S.D. Many of us do suffer from some of the symptoms of being exposed to S.D., but it is our disciplined mind that allows us to resist. The evidence is overwhelming. I ask you the next time you hear a politician condemn Cuba, China or Iran for torturing their prisoners, ask them about Pelikkkan Bay State Prison or Corcoran State Prison.

There's torture right here in Amerikkka. You can't tell me spending 30 years in solitary confinement or being exposed to sensory deprivation for the last 23 years is not torture. People, as you know, the CDCR has introduced a proposed solution and on paper it looks reasonable, but in practice it would not release the vast majority of us being housed in the Short Corridor. People, please don't allow yourselves to be deceived by forked tongues that slither across mouths that protrude from grotesque human-like caricatures that disguise themselves as correctional guards.

ABDUL OLUGBALA SHAKUR

Talk of Torture

I was recently asked to tell my story with regards to my experience of being tortured, especially being that many People within the u.s. do not believe that torture does take place in this country, a country that was built on the torturing of an entire race of People (e.g. Indigenous and Afrikan/New Afrikan People)!

I have had multiple experiences of being tortured especially back in the days. The one that I am often asked about is when they shot my testicles with the Taser over and over again.

I was placed in a unit called Bedrock, it was a unit initially designated for members of the Aryan Brotherhood (AB) when it first opened back in 1987, August the 7th, I was the only New Afrikan (Black) Prisoner placed in this unit at the time with 24 alleged members of the AB, an attempt by my keepers to get me murdered.

While in this unit I had got into it with a Black koon guard by the name of JJ, he was a Sgt., I called him a knee-grow koon, in response, he had me placed in 4 point restraints butt naked, and he placed a Taser on my testicles, telling me he will not stop until I call him Master or Daddy.

When Brothers asked me, why I refused to call him Master or Daddy so he can stop torturing me. I told these Brothers (none of these Brothers were Revolutionaries/Comrades), as a Revolutionary Guerrilla we are prepared to die before we surrender our Code of Honor to the enemy. Truthfully, I almost did called him Master, that shit was very painful, it was on the third day a white nurse came in the room and told them they would have to stop or she would report them. It was only a matter of time, I didn't yell, but they got some tears from my eyes, but I cursed them throughout the entire three days.

Please understand People, my experience is not an aberration, torture is occurring every single day within the u.s. Prison Industrial Slave-Complex (PISC). I am but one survivor, there are many, I do not seek your sympathy, for I am a New Afrikan Revolutionary, who freely give up my life for the People, so please do not cry for me, I just ask of you to support the New Afrikan Prison Movement. The Black Progress Prison Rights Movement.

CHAPTER

THREE

JOKA HESHIMA JINSAI

∿∿∿∿∿∿∿∿∿∿∿∿

The Antithesis of Oppression: How I Survived 20
Years of Solitary Confinement
29

JOKA HESHIMA JINSAI

The Antithesis of Oppression: How I Survived 20 Years of Solitary Confinement

"We are not contending with fools who will allow us to simply walk in and organize people to war against them. All serious challenges will be met with panic and repression."[1]
— George Jackson, *Blood in My Eye*

In recent months, renewed interest in the lives of those who were released to the mainline after decades in California's infamous SHU torture units has prompted many to ask us the question: "How did you survive decades of solitary confinement?" To understand how I survived almost two decades of solitary confinement, you must first understand why the state subjected us to these torture units in the first place.

The mistake many of us make in this culture is we often view things in their isolation as opposed to their interconnection. We experience social life through soundbites: tweets, Facebook posts and highly edited news clips, basing our social awareness on this narrow, easily manipulated view of the world.

This completely divorces us from the historical materialist ideology of social phenomena, and the many influences linked to that development. As a result, our perception of social and political reality rarely mirrors the truth.

Perhaps the single most poorly understood mechanism of the Amerikan social control apparatus is the purpose and function of solitary confinement. This misconception of its purpose and function – like misconceptions of other mechanisms of U.S. authoritarian institutions – is consistent with the fascist organization of U.S. society.

The purpose of contemporary solitary confinement "is to control revolutionary attitudes in prison systems and in the society at large,"[2] observed Ralph Aron, former warden of the Marion Control Unit.

It is a mechanism of social control with the specific political intent of destroying the sources of new ideas that possess the potential to transform the nature and structure of authoritarian society. Those who, in the state's determination, conform with such revolutionary ideas are condemned to this mechanism, designed to break the mind and further dehumanize us, in a society where torture already finds acceptance, as long as the state carries it out in service to "American interests and the public safety of the American people,"[3] according to former Secretary of Defense Donald Rumsfeld, speaking on enhanced interrogation techniques. Our minds, our social ties and our very humanity are targeted for eradication.

The U.S. domestic torture program carried out in SHU-style control units finds its origins at a meeting of social scientists and prison wardens held in Washington, D.C. in 1962. They adopted the findings of Dr. Edgar Schein, delivered in his presentation, "Man against Man: Brainwashing," as the basis of the program. In addressing the group, Dr. Schein stated: "I would like you to think of brainwashing, not in terms of politics, ethics or morals, but in terms of the deliberate changing of human behavior and attitudes by a group of men who have relatively complete control over the environment in which the captive population lives."[4]

To be effective, the techniques he espoused would require a new type of environment, conducive to altering the very foundations of one's perception of reality. For this, the state took Dr. Levinson's sensory deprivation prison unit design and a form of Skinnerian operant conditioning called "learned helplessness,"[5] and applied it to the very structure of SHUs.

Learned helplessness is a systematic process of conditioning, designed to crystalize in the imprisoned victim's mind that he has no control over the regulation of his existence and that he is helpless and must submit to the states power and control in order to "survive." In many ways, this process reflects the process of social conformity by the U.S. population to the dictates of capitalist society.

This, of course, runs contrary to core human consciousness and compels a linear thought divergence into two options: resistance or escape. The program is designed to apply the maximum punitive coercion against resistance and maximum pressure to explore the second option: escape. For those who are not immediately up for parole, there are only two escape options: debrief or die. To become broken men – or simply cease to exist.

I and those of like mind were placed in hell in indefinite solitary confinement *for decades*, based solely on our ideological adherence to New Afrikan Revolutionary Nationalism (NARN), our world view of revolutionary scientific socialism and our ardent desires to end oppression.

The reactionary response of the authoritarian state was to contain Revolutionary potential through repression, to delegitimize and criminalize it in hopes of diminishing its resonance amongst the prison population and society at large. Criminalizing labels like "gang member" and "terrorist" are joined with the isolation of other lumpen in order to criminalize legitimate revolutionaries by proxy. The characters of the two are falsely intertwined, to manufacture public acceptance of a practice which is wholly unacceptable in a humane society.

This point must be clear: The NARN prisoners in California were not consigned to indefinite solitary confinement because of any "criminal" act or "gang activity," but solely based on our political, social and cultural ideas and their transformative potential. We are unique in this regard.

But this does not truly encompass the depravity of the authoritarian state. Even our resistance was used against us. Those NARN prisoners capable of indefinite resistance to these torture techniques were held up as examples to the rest of the prison population of what fate awaits those following the path of principle, much as the Romans used crucifixion.

It served as such a powerful deterrent to ideological and political development for many that what I can only describe as a "philistine psychosis" has set in. Many New Afrikans avoided not only those who identify with NARN, but actually deride learning their own history and culture in general and the history and culture of New Afrikan resistance in particular for fear of a similar fate. That the state would subject us or others of like mind around the nation to decades of torture, with the express intent of breaking our minds in order to preclude the potential for the progressive transformation of U.S. society, exhibits its fascist character.

Nevertheless, in this crucible of concentrated repression, our wills *did not* wilt. Our purpose *did not* waiver. Our minds *did not* break. No, like a spear is plunged into the fire 10,000 times to hone the strongest blade, the crucible of torture only tempered my dedication to purpose. The SHU torture unit reveals the true nature of authoritarian society and those who govern it, offering a degree of clarity no amount of study or abstract political theorization could ever produce.

From the depths of this hell we reach forth to nurture and defend our communities, the people, and this world: an *absolute* commitment to end the oppression of Man and Woman, by man and woman. *This* is how I survived solitary confinement.

I survived solitary confinement by being transformed into its antithesis: the *New Afrikan Revolutionary Man*.

Instead of filling me with despair and resentment, it fueled my resistance and magnified my love and commitment to the poor oppressed masses who suffer from the cradle to the grave. For me, the torture unit acted as a window into the mind and heart of Amerika. It revealed a National character bent on absolute despotism and a heart as hollow as the void. Opposition to it requires us to give up our lives, so the origin of this evil is not allowed to spread unchecked.

I view my decades-long confinement in the SHU just as I do my recent release to general population. It's just the latest front in the same ever-evolving, 400-year-long struggle for freedom, justice and equality begun on the shores of Afrika, and continuing on the streets of capitalist Amerikkka.

There exists no greater expression of concentrated racism and absolute despotism in the U.S. capitalist arrangement than the indefinite solitary confinement unit. Dialectically, there exists no higher expression of humanity than the committed revolutionary. Not only does he continue to serve the people in spite of that repression, but he's constantly seeking ways to improve the quantity and quality of their service.

It was this dedication to purpose, this resolve to oppose tyranny, even while in its clutches, expressed by so many, which led to the organized resistance that paved our way to the prison mainline after so many years.

In the final analysis, it is the act of oppression, the deification of greed, the institutionalization of hate, and the imposition of unequal social, political and economic relationships which produce its opposite, the New Afrikan revolutionary. We exist because fascism, capitalism, racism, sexism, xenophobia, colonialism and imperialism compelled us to exist.

The fact that the fascist organization of society has legitimized the use of domestic torture units across the U.S. should not come as a great shock to any of us. Such brutal repression is consistent with the history of America.

From the horror of the slave ships to the "Strange Fruit" of the Jim Crow South, violence is the underlying basis of power and profit in Amerikan society. But that repression always breeds its antithesis: Nat Turner, Denmark Vessey, Gabriel Prosser, Harriet Tubman, Bunchy Carter, W.L. Nolen and so many others who came into being as living embodiments of resistance to this evil.

That legacy has not passed from us. We will always come into being, so long as freedom, justice and equality do not shine down on all of humanity like a star in the night. Revolutionary resistance, transformative opposition to this system of hate, is the very foundation of the survival of New Afrikan people in this age who want to see themselves free of the evils and injustice of capitalism.

I, and those of like mind, will continue to survive, continue to fight on, continue to serve the people, so long as this system exists, and beyond. We will *never* surrender, *never* give up, *never* give in, and in the end, we will win.

Think on these things. They are cause for great meditation.

Until we win, or don't lose.

CHAPTER

FOUR

ABDUL OLUGBALA SHAKUR

ABDUL OLUGBALA SHAKUR

Humanity Indicted For Our Silence In the Face of Torture

As imprisoned activists we've often asked society: *What have your eyes seen to wish to see no more? And what have your ears heard to wish to hear no more?*

Your self-imposed silence has only fueled the government's thirst for fascist repression, and this repression has manifested on every level of society, causing humanity to hemorrhage, while debris from this hemorrhaging stains the dissipating remnants of a deteriorating society.

People, I don't intend to be poetic, but it is imperative that this indictment tap into the depths of your rhythmic soul, with the hope that we are able to reawaken your true sense of humanity and restore your hearing and sight, so you can hear our voices and see a society that is trapped within its own sins!

Some may even find the above paragraphs contextually out of place at first glance, but it is a prerequisite, necessitated by a society that for the most part has lost its moral vision as well as its capacity of humane discernment, compelling us to ponder over the possibility that our words will fall upon deaf ears. What was once morally reprehensible is now immorally acceptable and justified under particular situations or circumstances, thus leaving humanity and justice at the dictate of a subjective scrutiny.

We can no longer assume that we are speaking to a society that is firmly rooted in the tenets of an ethical constitution, especially when the evidence of an impaired moral fortitude appears to permeate every level of social stratification. So our question to ourselves as imprisoned activists and embedded reporters for the people:

How do we articulate a moral indictment on the subject of torture that is capable of penetrating the exterior periphery of a post 9/11 culture, where torture for the most part is no longer considered a crime or an act against humanity, but rather a tool to extract information – intelligence – or a weapon designed to censor, persecute, punish and ideologically subdue the imprisoned activists and embedded reporters?

Or a governmental strategy designed to suppress the poor communities, the New Afrikan community in particular?

Articulating the diabolical anatomy of torture for a post 9/11 society is no doubt a task that must be diligently executed, for it is too important an issue to allow subjective sentiments to cause us to neglect our responsibility as imprisoned activists. We are still obligated to serve. Even a morally decadent society is deserving of saving – yes, even if those doing the saving are imprisoned activists!

When we speak about the anatomy of torture, this inherently encompasses its socio-political, socio-cultural and spiritual ramifications. The government deliberately omits this aspect of torture, which is the most pertinent and significant element. But the government also understands it is this very element that has the potential to ignite societal and spiritual expostulation, impeding their ability to use torture as a political tool, both domestically and globally.

Most people, including the so-called experts, tend to perpetuate a fundamental and erroneous interpretation of torture. People often perceive physical and psychological torture as two separate entities. Their hypothesis implies physical torture is exclusively physical, and psychological torture is exclusively psychological.

Contrary to this popular myth, their practical applications and execution explicitly imply that both physical and psychological torture is one and the same, though with two distinguishable components. But in practice, they are constantly interchanging, morphing into one another, where the physical becomes the psychological or vice versa!

Psychological torture has a physical characteristic. Those under the subjugation of psychological torture also experience physical torture – pain. Psychological torture unquestionably produces an intense stress that eventually wreaks havoc on the body, turning the body on itself. Physical torture also possesses a psychological characteristic.

Before we discuss the subject of torture, let's first be clear on what it is. Many people within the poor community look at torture one dimensionally, not even realizing that they are constantly under the subjugation of government-sponsored torture. For example: When the cops murder an unarmed Black male or murder a 12-year-old Black manchild, this is a form of torture – using government-sponsored violence as a tool of both psychological and physical torture. These acts of blatant terrorism are designed to instill fear into our community. Every time we step outside of our homes, the threat of government-sponsored violence is always present, producing stress, which affects our physical health.

Post-9/11 made torture an acceptable evil, not only in the U.S. government's so-called war on terrorism, but also the government's domestic deployment of torture. Not that this is a new phenomenon, but its social acceptance among some segments of society is new, and this radical change unfortunately became the catalyst for the Prison Industrial Slave Complex (PISC) to rapidly increase its torture program with impunity!

It is not even a question that both physical and psychological torture is a constant reality throughout the Prison Industrial Slave Complex; the issue that presently confronts us is the widespread acceptance of our torture. Are we not even considering the moral and social ramifications of a society that has lost its humanity?

And then you wonder how could a police officer murder a 12-year-old Black manchild? Or a 70-year-old sista? Or a 6-year-old womanchild? The social acceptance of torture domestically or globally should serve as an indictment of the absence of our collective sense of humanity – a society that is slowly dying and doesn't even know it.

Do you think that God accepts or tolerates our daily torture in his name? Do you not know that you as a member of this society will one day have to answer for turning a deaf ear and a blind eye to the cry of human suffering at the hands of *government-sponsored torture*?
I ask you to pray on this, if you are a true believer, for your humanity is under indictment. Put your hands up! Your humanity has no right to remain silent. Speak out against torture!

ABDUL OLUGBALA SHAKUR

A Solitary Distinction

Since our historical release from solitary confinement, many of us have been bombarded by the same question: How did you (we) survive decades of being in solitary confinement? This is not a question of simplicity; it is only a qualitative and quantitative prelude into an analysis rooted in a historical material construct which would require a compartmentalization of the particulars which are conducive towards providing an accurate response to the above question with both clarity and purpose.

Not to diminish the suffering that other races and/or classes were subjugated to while in solitary confinement, but it would be a grave injustice for anyone to censor from this state-sponsored atrocity that the New Afrikan Revolutionary Nationalist prisoners were placed and retained in solitary confinement for revolutionary political activities and their strong beliefs in justice for our people, not for criminal drugs or gang activities.

We were being politically and racially persecuted, and our treatment was in fact different and exclusive to our New Afrikan

Revolutionary Collective, in which our New Afrikan Revolutionary brothas and sistas across the country were and are experiencing the same exact state-sponsored repression – COINTELPRO in disguise. As many of our New Afrikan Revolutionary brothas and sistas across the country can and will attest, we must keep our political torture and detention in its proper perspective and not allow it to be convoluted with the general discussion on this topic.

Before there was a Pelikkkan Bay State Prison, hunger strikes or a class action lawsuit, our New Afrikan Revolutionary Nationalist (NARN) Collective was basically alone in this fight against state-sponsored repression, racism and racially motivated violence. No one or group has lost or suffered more than our Revolutionary Collective.

Though we have not been perfect in our service, no single individual, group or organization has sacrificed or been more persecuted than our NARN Collective for preserving, protecting and promoting the legacy of Comrade George L. Jackson.

Though we have suffered alone and we have *never* asked for sympathy nor pity, we pound our chest and spit fire in the spirit of those who came before us. Though we don't receive the credit nor recognition we rightfully deserve, I, as one proud New Afrikan Revolutionary Nationalist, extend my most profound and unconditional love, trust, respect and support to our NARN Collective from California to New York, to those who have stayed true to our revolutionary creed.

The above statement, though brief, is critical towards understanding our answer to the question: How did we survive decades in solitary confinement?

We do not define survival based on how an individual has effectively preserved his or her sanity while in solitary confinement. We define survival based on the restoration of one's sense of humanity and a dedication towards improving this world for our children and people to live in!

You have not survived when you return back to the same self-destructive behaviors that were part of your life prior to being placed in solitary confinement; your self-imposed relapse is indicative of your defeat! After all one has endured, how can one engage in any activity or behavior that facilitate recidivism or the destabilization of one's community? This is not surviving solitary confinement!

For our NARN Collective, the struggle is far from over. Being in general population has only magnified the difficulties of our revolutionary task. In 2015, the city of Chicago had approximately 763 homicides and over 4,000 shootings, and at least 95 percent of those victims were New Afrikans.

This is what weighs on the minds and hearts of our NARN Collective. And being able to contribute towards the resolution of this contradiction – i.e., without working with the pigs or government – is indicative towards our survival and the preservation and affirmation of our sense of humanity!

I had promised to keep this brief, but at times the fire that burns in the depths of my raging soul pushes forward like an uncontrollable wave of lava, scorching any attempts to restrain the blood that flows from eyes that have seen too much.

But before I put my pen to rest, allow me to extend unconditional love, respect, trust and support to Sista Mary and Brotha Willie Ratcliff, for they have sacrificed more than most of us can even imagine in their support for us. We owe them, and it should be our obligatory duty to mobilize our support and resources to ensure the continuity and longevity of the Bay View newspaper and protect it from cowardly busters.

I must equally extend my unconditional New Afrikan Revolutionary love, trust, respect and support to Kilaika Shakur, Akili Mwalimu Shakur, Bomani Jihad Shakur, Anajaku Cole, Brotha Kasim, Mabu Shakur, Malik Jamaa Shakur, Rafiki Jemel, my spiritual father Dr. Donald R. Evans, and the GJU Collective – www.GeorgeJacksonUniversity.com, GJU Radio at 347-826-7332 every Wednesday 5-7 p.m., and the Black August Organizing Committee (BAOC), and special love to my wife, Sharifa Dafina Shakur, and Azadeh Zohrabi for her unconditional support.

I will now answer the question: How did I survive 32 ½ years in solitary confinement? I survived with "Blood in My Eye," while writing prison letters, during "The Art of War," wrapped around "The Isis Papers" for "Two Thousand Seasons," resisting the "Destruction of Black Civilization," while "Breaking the Chains of Psychological Slavery," with "Negroes With Guns," being navigated by the "Appeals of David Walker," while the "Melancholy History of Soledad" revealed the "Agents of Repression."

But "The Dragon Has Come" with the "Introduction to Afrikan Civilization," as I find solace and true Black love and beauty with "Assata." Now you know how I survived 32½ years in solitary confinement under both racial and political repression and persecution! War without terms – power to those who don't fear freedom! Death before dishonor!

CHAPTER

FIVE

ABDUL OLUGBALA SHAKUR

olooolooloolo

Chess vs Checkers

Life is like a game of chess and checkers. Many of us play checkers. And many of us think we're playing chess, but, in practice, we're actually playing checkers. So it should be of no surprise to any of you when I say, most poor people play checkers, prisoners in particular.

Now what does this analogy imply? Most people make decisions in life without thinking ahead or assessing the ramifications of their decisions, especially prisoners! When I was asked to write about the End of Hostilities Agreement and our future direction(s) and plans, I chose to employ the chess and checkers analogy as a vehicle to expedite my task. Most prisoners understand the basic principles of chess, and this is one of the reasons I chose to utilize this analogy.

The End of Hostilities Agreement is rooted in the matrix of a strategic alliance. What this ultimately means: We have long term objectives with short terms necessities. The hunger strike was a short term necessity, while the end to long term solitary confinement, SHU, gang validation and debriefing was our strategic goal. But the inherent element that had complemented the amalgamation of the diversity of race, culture, ideology and personality was our capacity to require that we think in terms of chess, not checkers!

Our keepers have the mentality of a checker player, and it was this disposition that allowed us to outmaneuver CDCr, for we were and are many steps ahead of them. They think one move at a time. It is CDCr's arrogance that prevents them from seeing us as intellectual equals. I believe that our success via the hunger strike, as well as the class-action lawsuit, have forced our keepers to reevaluate their perception of our collective here in the Short Corridor – thus, the introduction of the new regulations pertaining to obscene material.

CDCr's reaction to our success is indicative of their checker mentality, not thinking ahead, but rather one move at a time. A chess player would have foreseen the potentiality of future class-action lawsuits.

Simplifying the complexities of my complicated endeavor would no doubt facilitate readers' capacity to intellectually digest the textual content of my intent and purpose for composing this communique. We as an imprisoned class are trying to encourage our fellow prisoners to think like chess players and understand that our success lies with our ability and capacity to think strategically.

Race riots derive from checker mentalities, antiquated and primitive responses to contradictions that can clearly be resolved by thinking before reacting. What is our best move? In the May, 2014 issue of the Bay View newspaper, the New Afrikan activist, Joe A'Jene Valentine, in his article "Review Board Suggests Pelican Bay Prisoner Stop Political Writing for Favorable Placement," eloquently assesses the anatomy of a race riot. For example, when he had correctly identified the sources of the vast majority of so-called race riots, he wrote:

> In truth, most of the conflicts between Blacks and Southern Mexicans or New Afrikans and North Amerikans/Whites are motivated by drug or gambling debts or street gang shit. Upon close examination of such conflicts in the tombs, it will be discovered that, in the main, these aren't inherently 'racial conflicts.' If they were,

Blacks and Northern Mexicans would be in conflict.[1]

—Joe A'Jene Valentine

There exists more relevant and powerful assessments within the content of Brotha A'Jene's article, but I will stop here, for in the above analysis A'Jene clearly identified two of the principal factors that can be attributed to race riots. They have nothing to do with race but more to do with an antiquated prison culture and gang psychology.

It is true that the majority of so-called race riots are in fact precipitated by drug deals gone bad, gambling debts and the matter of disrespect, all of which can be resolved via the chess mentality. For example: A brotha should not engage in any illicit activities, such as gambling, across culture or color lines. The potential for a racial conflict is too great to take that chance.

This is thinking before one makes a move – to question what are the consequences or potential consequences of my actions? This cross-culture or cross-color gambling can potentially lead to a conflict between Black and Mexican or White prisoners, where there exists the strong possibility of prisoners being hurt, if not killed! And for what? Because I want to gamble with a prisoner of another race?

A chess thinker would forbid prisoners from engaging in any activity that has the potential to break out into a conflict between different racial or rival groups. This is a true leader, a chess player having the foresight to see and understand what is in the best interest of his or her race or group!

Think about this: Let's say during one of those conflicts one of your homeboys gets shot or killed. Who do you hold accountable – keeping in mind how this conflict started? Over a gambling debt? Drugs? As chess thinkers, we value the lives of those who we claim as our comrades, brothas, homeboys, so whatever decisions we make must encompass an assessment of their outcome.

Calipatria Prison is obviously a prison full of checker players, not thinking before they move, reacting without assessing the consequences of their actions, not realizing that their actions are having far reaching implications, playing right into the hands of the guards, undermining all the hard work we are putting in to put an end to long-term solitary confinement, censorship, brutality, isolation, medical negligence, torture and other CDCr-sanctioned crimes. (But since that story, prisoners at Calipatria have been reading the End of Hostilities Agreement and heeding it).

We understood the key to our success was our non-violent protest. This is why our keepers did everything in their power to provoke a violent response from us. But their tricks did not work. We held fast to our resolve. We calculated our every move and those of our fascist keepers, staying at least five moves ahead. And as a result, we have won multiple battles, but the war is far from being over. Each move we make is designed for the end-game – checkmate! – but it is the checker players who impede our forward progress.

I believe if the checker players understood the end-game they would adopt the principles of the chess players, for it is within this knowledge that our common goals are exemplified: 1) Abolish the Prison Industrial Slave Complex (PISC), 2) Abolish the Security Housing Unit (SHU) and put an end to long-term solitary confinement, 3) Put an end to torture, 4) Put an end to the death penalty, 5) Eradicate recidivism!

As New Afrikan imprisoned freedom fighters, one of our primary goals is to stabilize our communities. At present, it is the instability of our communities that facilitates the path from poverty to crime to prison. It is the fuel which feeds the PISC, so it becomes an imperative prerequisite for us to go beyond the PISC with our agenda.

The End of Hostilities Agreement is also applicable to our communities. This is an example of our chess mentality. We are thinking 10 moves ahead, beyond our immediate environment, for we understand the relation between the conditions in our communities and the survival of the PISC.

An individual once told me that he believed that he can beat me in a game of chess, and I told him this may be true, but the difference between you and me: Your game is trapped within the 64 squares on the chess board. The goal is to show you how to transfer your chess game from the game board to the game of life, and the game of life is much bigger than concrete and steel – or drugs and gambling. These things only have a quasi-value on a checker board but are worthless in the game of life.

People, this communique is not only applicable to the prisoner class. I am equally speaking to the community at large. The checker mentality permeates the oppressed class on every level, the New Afrikan community in particular. It impedes our growth and development as a people and community. It contaminates our sense of priorities.

We have to think beyond the checker board. Every move we make must be examined and re-examined: How will this decision affect me, my family, my community and my people?

The most powerful weapon we have is on our neck. We are armed with the capacity to build the new pyramids of the 21st century, and we must not allow ourselves to be disarmed by the game of checkers!

Power to the people who don't fear freedom!

(Note: Unbeknownst to many, even prison rights activists, Brotha Abdul Olugbala Shakur develop the original blueprint to the "End of Hostility Agreement").

ABDUL OLUGBALA SHAKUR

The Death Penalty: Killing in the Name of God is the Ultimate Act of Blasphemy

The Death Penalty is one of many signs of a society that is morally deteriorating, especially a society that proclaims an affinity with God and the Holy Scriptures. First of all, there's nothing in the Holy Scriptures which gives moral support and/or credence to the implementation of the Death Penalty. This is a man-made evil, and it is this spiritual contradiction that will eventually condemn us all to a spiritual and moral death.

This is a moral and spiritual issue, and being thus, it is imperative for society at large to analyze the social and moral dynamics pertaining to the Death Penalty from a perspective that magnifies and values human life – humanity – for its social and moral implications are beginning to manifest within the norm of societal behavior and attitudes.

For example, at every execution there is always a crowd of people who are proponents of the Death Penalty standing outside the prison gates cheering the execution of the condemned. Many of them often have signs jokingly mocking the human life that is about to be taken in the name of man's warped sense of justice.

This celebration of death, of state-sponsored homicide, in many instances is carried out right before the family and children of the condemned. They shout out, "Kill the bastard!" completely oblivious to the impact their venomous hate is going to have on these children.

I have witnessed on a number of occasions these proponents of the Death Penalty direct their venom towards the children of the condemned, children who are hours away from being without a father. It is unfortunate that most people are not able to recognize the implications of these confrontations but, more poignantly, many of them appear not to care as they are caught up in a bloodletting frenzy orchestrated by the government and law enforcement.

Rather than create laws that are designed to encourage forgiveness, compassion and fairness, the government chose to orchestrate a social climate that incites the fallible, primeval nature of mankind when violent aggression was man's expression of recompense. This is not by accident.

In order for the Death Penalty to become an acceptable practice within a professedly democratic society that claims to be founded upon the Holy Scriptures, the government had to reconstruct the societal psychosis in a way that it would become more susceptible to draconian governmental laws for dispensing so-called justice.

I realize that the very implications of my accusatorial proclamation sounds incredible, but allow me to elaborate: A perfect analogy that I believe would both facilitate and convey my assessment is how the government orchestrated the social climate in California to help pass the state three-strikes law. This law was already lying on the political shelf because the government understood that most California taxpayers would oppose the implementation of the three-strikes law, so they never introduced it at the time it was originally presented to them by an individual whose daughter was murdered.

But when 10-year-old Polly Klaas was viciously raped and murdered by a repeat offender, it rapidly altered the socio-political climate.

Via the media, the government and law enforcement bombarded the people of California with images of this little girl's dead body, and the criminal history of the sick individual who murdered and raped this precious little girl. This enraged the people – and rightfully so.

The conditions were now ripe for the introduction of the three-strikes law. This law was presented as a law designed to protect our children from sexual predators, and the people had no reason to disbelieve the government.

But the government and law enforcement knew from the outset this law had nothing to do with protecting our children from sexual predators. They had intentionally exploited the violent torture and death of a little girl to incite and solicit the emotions – the rage – of the people to make this racist law more acceptable.

As we all know, when humans become emotional, they tend to overlook details. Now the true intentions of the three-strikes law have revealed themselves, but the damage has been done. Even though efforts are being initiated to mitigate the damage, it is too late.

The Death Penalty is another example. It is not a deterrent, but a government-sponsored medium to exact societal revenge, and we as a people are the primary target of that societal retribution laced with racial hate.

People, I do understand your fear, anger and frustration, but it is these extreme emotions which often impair our moral vision and corrupt our sense of spiritual awareness, and the Death Penalty is clear example of that impaired moral vision.

Once a society loses its moral vision, it becomes subjugated to the plagues of human atrocity after human atrocity, unable to stop the self-destructive cycle. What was once unacceptable now becomes the norm. I ask what have your eyes seen to wish to see no more?

The moral and social ramifications of the implementation of the Death Penalty permeate all levels of this society. Even the family of the victim(s) equate the closure of their personal loss with the execution of the accused. In some states, the government is making it a victim's right for the family of the deceased to be present at the execution of the accused; and many of the politicians are elected into office simply because they advocate for the Death Penalty, the legalization of government-sponsored murder.

I ask once again: What have your eyes seen to wish to see no more? Must I dare ask, are we worthy of the Garden of Eden? Not only did we eat the apple; we planted the damn tree! It is symbolic of our spiritual and moral demise.

I often wonder, for those who believe in heaven, how does one explain to God the execution of an innocent person? Or even how does one justify one's thirst for revenge? Are these qualities of a Christian?

Will this heaven have a Death Penalty? Will the Prophet Muhammad, Moses and Abraham be part of the firing squad? Or would Jesus be required to insert the lethal injection? Oh, I almost forgot; only man has the honor to execute another human being, for we have yet to provide this human privilege to God and his Prophets.

I ask for you to open up your Holy Qur'an, Holy Bible or Holy Torah and whisper to your sense of humanity: What have your eyes seen to wish to see no more? And what have your ears heard to wish to hear no more?

Has God capitulated his will to man? No! He has not! Mankind has raped our beloved God of his true virtues. The devil must be very proud of mankind, for we have mastered the art of killing in the name of God – the ultimate act of blasphemy!

CHAPTER

SIX

ABDUL OLUGBALA SHAKUR

ᕣᕠᕓᕟᕣᕠᕓᕟᕣᕠᕓᕟ

ABDUL OLUGBALA SHAKUR

From Slavery to Suicide

A common denominator among individuals who commit suicide is a traumatic event and/or long-term torment which can result in psychosis. If left untreated, it can lead to suicidal thoughts with the intent to end the internal distress and anguish. This same diagnostic assessment is equally applicable to mass suicide.

I believe that we as a people are trying to commit mass suicide by proxy, and we live in a society, a world, that is only too willing to provide us with all the means to facilitate our collective unconscious suicidal aspirations. I realize that many of you will no doubt vehemently challenge my hypothesis. I myself was initially reluctant to accept my own thesis, but our day to day reality confirms it.

Before I expound on my thesis, allow me to briefly distract you and direct your attention to an observation I believe is very pertinent towards affirming its validity.

When the Jews came out of their Holocaust, they pledged *never again!* The state of Israel is indicative of that pledge, and one societal aspect that both resonates and epitomizes that pledge more than anything else is their law of conscription. Every Jewish citizen, when he or she turns 18, must join and serve at least two to three years in the armed forces, creating a people and society that is armed with both the skill and means to defend itself.

But when we as a people came out of our Holocaust – i.e., genocidal slavery and Jim Crow – our pledge was not *never again*. We pledged to participate in our own genocide via integration, assimilation and acculturation before we could even fully recover, while the Jews' priority was to restore their national and racial identity and consolidate their forces before they decided to integrate within the global community.

In contrast, our priority was to completely surrender both our racial and national identity without restoring our original Afrikan psyche. For the most part we as a people did not make that pledge, *never again*. We pledged to sacrifice everything innately Afrikan-centric to become an offspring of a Euro-centric construct with a DNA to serve others while blindly determined to destroy ourselves. Our social reality tends to substantiate this observation.

My people, we should have pledged *never again*! And not, can I sit on the front of your bus, or sit at your lunch counter, or participate in your corrupted political system! And we're still wondering why we find ourselves trapped in this constant cycle of poverty and death? You may ask: What does this have to do with my hypothesis of our collective suicidal ambitions?

Well, I can identify many visible symptoms that would illuminate explicit signs of mass suicide, but I will use this opportunity to briefly explicate the most proliferated and transparent symptom of mass suicide that even the most stoic skeptics cannot deny. I realize many of our people may find the tendency to amalgamate the external with the internal – i.e., the genocide with the suicide – which I agree is critical towards comprehending the totality of the reality of our situation, but what is equally imperative is identifying our contribution: Our unconscious suicidal aspirations complement the White supremacist's conscious aspirations to commit genocide on our race.

As I previously stated, there are a number of symptoms that we can identify that would support my hypothesis of our collective participation in our mass suicide attempt, but I will identify only the three that permeate our communities the most. The leading causes of death that we have complete control over are 1) Black-on-Black gang violence, 2) heart disease, and 3) HIV/AIDS – all symptomatic of a race trying to commit suicide. (Note, I did not neglect the impact abortion is having on the rapid reduction of our population. I wanted to use this opportunity to focus on the above-listed three.)

I agree that there exist a number of collateral symptoms that are equally conducive towards both our unconscious suicidal aspirations and the conscious genocidal agenda that we have been subjugated to since our forced arrival upon these shores as Afrikan slaves. For example, the mass incarceration of our people, our inability to defend ourselves against racial violence and oppression, the mass unemployment, an ineffective school system, the absence of New Afrikan fathers in many homes. All these elements deserve to be identified as symptoms, but the theme of this thesis is the three primary symptoms that contribute to thousands of New Afrikan/Black deaths annually.

One of my comrades asked am I implying that our people are unconsciously suicidal by nature? I told him not by nature, but by orientation. We have become unconsciously suicidal, a psychosis directly associated to our historical miscarriage – i.e., the Black Holocaust – a generational psychosis that for the most part has been left untreated. As a result we have developed an inherent collective propensity for engaging in self-destructive behavior with little to no discernment of its devastating ramifications.

Thousands of our young people are dying annually due to Black-on-Black gang violence and we tend to accept this as the norm. Hundreds if not thousands of our young people contract HIV/AIDS annually, but yet our young people continue to engage in unprotected sex. Thousands of our people die annually as a result of heart disease, yet we still eat unhealthily. Obesity is an epidemic in our communities, and we have yet to take control of our blood pressure or high cholesterol.

We are killing ourselves at an alarming rate, and it appears that we have become completely anesthetized to the harsh reality of our situation, relishing in our own extinction, because despite the obvious symptoms of a suicidal fate, we continue to move forward ever more destructive to ourselves and community with each passing year. Black death is cheap, not only in Amerikkka but globally.

My people, I tend to direct my words primarily to our people and community. I believe too often we speak about how we are treated as people – and rightfully so – but our suffering will only end when we take responsibility for how we respond to our oppression. The key to our success lies within our collective ability to aggressively but strategically respond to any external threat and/or internal turmoil, from unemployment to pig brutality.

I ask, do you know your nearest New Afrikan neighborhood? If not, why not? Do you check on the elders in your community? If not, why not? Do you watch over the neighborhood children while they play outdoors? If not, why not? I can go on and on, but the point I'm making: The power lies with us to put an end to our self-destructive behavior and effectively resist the forces of oppression.

Are my words falling on deaf ears? I must ask: Is slicing our wrist any different from having unprotected sex? Is jumping off a bridge any different from consuming large amounts of salt and fatty foods daily in spite of our high blood pressure and high cholesterol? Is Black-on-Black gang violence any different from putting a gun to our head and pulling the damn trigger?

Our unconscious suicidal aspirations are but a manifested symptom of a psychosis that was born out of 400 years of racial persecution. But is there a cure? My beloved people, as your New Afrikan legal combatant, I am here to tell you that there is a cure for this psychosis – for it dwells within the spirit of Harriet Tubman, Nat Turner, David Walker, Denmark Vesey, Sojourner Truth, Ida B.

Wells, George Jackson, Bunchy Carter, Assata Shakur, Nehanda Abiodun.

The cure equally lies within our Afrikan-centric roots, the unity and support for one another, the unconditional love for ourselves and our people. I sincerely invite you to drink of this cup of resistance, Black Power and Black Natural Beauty!

Willie Lynch Syndrome

Before I proceed, we can all concede to the fact that there is a strong probability that the Willie Lynch letter is a hoax and that there exists no credible documented evidence that Willie Lynch even existed, though some claim Frederick Douglass once made reference to Willie Lynch. So not to get in a quagmire or distracted in the debate over the validity of the Willie Lynch letter, we can all unequivocally concede that within the context of that hoax letter there exist factual descriptions of some of the methods that were actually employed by slave masters and kolonialists across the country and the world. It is these documented methods that we call the Willie Lynch System.

I choose to use the title the Willie Lynch System to facilitate the content of this message with the hope of illuminating how these methods are being applied in the 21st century. These methods are still a functional stratagem within the ideology of kapitalism, though they are often inconspicuous within society. But within the prison industrial slave-complex, the 21st century plantation, these methods are magnified tenfold and the wardens serve as the slave masters overseeing their concrete plantations.

The slave masters had developed and executed a multitude of methods designed to preserve the proliferation and longevity of the genocidal slave system, and the wardens throughout the country have implemented a number of similar methods within their government-sanctioned concrete plantations, but my focus here is to briefly illustrate a method that was designed to discourage Black prisoners from relinquishing their criminal mentality and becoming New Afrikan Revolutionaries.

During the years of genocidal slavery, the slave master would identify the most rebellious and incorrigible Black slave and whip and beat him to death in front of all the other slaves as a vivid reminder of the severe consequences for resisting the will of the slave master. The warden overseers have incorporated a similar method, but a modified application to meet the new set of circumstances and goals, and the Prison Industrial Slave Complex is one of the leading pioneers in the advancement of the Willie Lynch System and methods.

Within the scope of their operational deployment, the execution aspects are less brutal, but brutal nonetheless, and just as effective. Within the realm of the Prison Industrial Slave Complex, the warden overseer and his/her agents – e.g., Office of Correctional Safety (OCS), Institutional Gang Investigations Unit (IGI), Investigative Services Unit (ISU) – identify those New Afrikan revolutionary prisoners who they fear possess the potential to transform the Black criminal mentality into a revolutionary mentality and place them (us) in solitary confinement and then subject them to a number of torturous tactics designed to both break our will and serve as a warning to discourage Black prisoners from making that transformation.

Wardens and their gang investigators identify those New Afrikan revolutionary prisoners who they fear possess the potential to transform the Black criminal mentality into a revolutionary mentality and place them (us) in solitary confinement and then subject them to a number of torturous tactics designed to both break our will and serve as a warning to discourage Black prisoners from making that transformation.

In order for us to fully grasp the significance of the modified application of the Willie Lynch System – based on our definition of the Willie Lynch System (WLS) – in the 21st century, we must first identify its present goal(s). During the era of genocidal slavery the slave masters employed the WLS to facilitate and guarantee the continuity of Afrikan slavery. The warden-overseers' objective is similar. Their goal is to preserve the Black criminal mentality to guarantee Black recidivism to facilitate that path from the hood to prison.

My people, we are losing thousands of our young people annually due to Black-on-Black gang violence and thousands monthly due to mass incarceration. Our communities are like factories producing raw commodities – human commodities – to fuel the PISC. We cannot effectively abolish the PISC (Prison Industrial Slave Complex) without addressing those conditions which are conducive towards fueling the PISC, such as Black-on-Black violence.

We can resolve the epidemic of violence and criminal survival in our communities without working with the pigs, government or the Prison Industrial Slave Complex. The New Afrikan Revolutionary Prisoners understand this crisis better than anyone and the warden overseers are aware of this and this explains their oppressive campaign against our New Afrikan Revolutionary Collective nationwide. Our isolation and the censoring of our voice and political views, as well as our torture, are designed to interfere with our endeavors to transform the Black criminal mentality.

My beloved people, it is critical to our success that we as a people understand the systems that we are up against. Our plans often fail because we lack a practical comprehension of that which oppresses us. Though we can concede that the Willie Lynch letter was a hoax, no one can deny the methods that were described in that hoax letter were factual. This is well documented and we need not have to debate with any 21st century house slaves to confirm the validity of these methods.

When our New Afrikan girls identify the White doll with beauty and the Black doll with ugly, this is clearly indicative of self-hate. There exist hundreds if not thousands of living examples that can and will confirm the validity of these methods described in the Willie Lynch letter. Though we are over a hundred years removed from genocidal slavery, we are still suffering the ramifications of an enslaved and tortured people. We have yet to fully recover. Just because many of our people have succeeded – according to their individual definition of success – does not negate the psychological effects or the existence of the methods employed by the slave masters that we now choose to call the Willie Lynch System.

During the years of slavery, there were over 2,000 documented Black slave masters, but this fact does not abrogate the fact that the U.S. system of genocidal slavery was a racist-based construct, and this is still applicable today. Our success or liberation will not be determined by the Negro Kapitalist, neo-Kolonialist upper and middle class. Our success and freedom will be determined by the New Afrikan oppressed under-Klass, not by a knee-grow minority, nor shall we allow the Black Kapitalist to define our truths and realities!

Before I end this text, it would be remiss of me to neglect to make the following declaration: It is imperative that we thoroughly understand that there exists a connection between the Prison Industrial Slave Complex and the ills that inflict our communities, such as gang violence, and that we can't abolish the PISC without resolving those ills which are destabilizing our communities. This would necessitate a concerted effort.

We must support one another tangibly.

We need to get past all the unnecessary feel-good rhetoric and begin to work on a pragmatic, practical and collective agenda designed to get the job done. Our support for one another must become more tangible, beyond hollow words. For example:

1. The Bay View must become the people's voice. We spend – i.e., waste – money buying subscriptions to magazines that only promote Kapitalism with a Black face, such as Ebony, Essence and Black Enterprise – plantation periodicals. The Bay View speaks to our culture of resistance, justice and freedom. A voice for the unheard.

I am compelled to ask, when was the last time a subscription to Ebony, Essence or XXL saved the lives of our children? When was the last time spending over $100 for a pair of Nikes stopped Black-on-Black gang violence?

When was the last time a $400 weave prevented teenage pregnancy or the spread of HIV/AIDS? I ask, why are we so eager to invest our money into those things that are of no moral or cultural value – while allowing those things, such as the Bay View, that are of great value to go unfunded? Is this not a profile of a damned slave? The Willie Lynch letter may be a hoax but the methods are more real today than they were back then. We think and act as if we're inferior, not our true selves. We have no sense of priority as a community, but we are quick to blame racism for our failure to act responsibly.

The Bay View must become the heart and soul of the New Afrikan Black underclass. We must mobilize our energy and resources to guarantee its longevity and pledge our support to Willie and Mary Ratcliff and Brotha JR in their endeavors to make the Bay View the heartbeat of the people's movement and true New Afrikan egalitarianism.

As I have always, I must ask: What have your eyes seen to wish to see no more? And what have your ears heard to wish to hear no more? Can deafness and blindness be our collective desire? Can you hear beyond your own voice, or see beyond your own vision? Have we become that mentally handicapped where we have lost our natural capacity to grasp our true sense of humanity? Have we fallen that far where we are no longer able to find our true self? What have we done for you to ask no more?

2. I ask: How serious are you about resolving the Black-on-Black
    gang violence, recidivism? Then you must go beyond just
    expressing your frustration. I encourage you to tap into the
    people's think tank where we are committed to solving the
    problems that confront our communities.

At present we are developing a revolutionary think tank
completely dedicated to building strong and self-sufficient
communities. We are solution-oriented beyond hollow rhetoric and
revolutionary slogans. This think tank will consist of New Afrikan
(Black) community activists, New Afrikan scholars and students and
New Afrikan revolutionary prisoners. Together we can and will make
a positive difference.

Our revolutionary think tank is known as the Bunchy Carter
Institute for Revolutionary Change (BCIRC). Our present goal is to
get more community activists and students involved in the BCIRC.

Let's say an activist or parent is interested in addressing the gang
issue in their community. They can send their question or concerns to
the Bay View and this is why it is imperative for the community to
support the Bay View, the only national newspaper that provides
lifesaving and life-sustaining service to the New Afrikan community.

My people, we can't keep living off the ancient glories of our
ancestors. What form of pyramids are we going to leave behind? Our
communities should become the pyramids of the 21st century and not
the ruins of ancient past. As New Afrikan political prisoners and
POWs, and politically conscious prisoners, we will never capitulate to
the trappings of the Willie Lynch System, but our light can and will
shine much brighter if we connect as one for this common cause. I
reiterate; we can't keep blaming racism for our own failure to do
what's in our own best interest. I now bid you peace and solidarity.

ABDUL OLUGBALA SHAKUR

We Pledged to Become Martyrs to Force CDCR to the Negotiating Table

While at California State Prison-Sacramento (New Folsom), we had received word that the CDCR was refusing to negotiate our hunger strike demands with the four main reps (prisoner representatives), so myself and two other New Afrikans pledged to become martyrs with the intent of forcing the CDCR to the negotiating table. I decided it would make more of an impact if I go first.

Approximately August 28th we had stopped taking the vitamins or drinking the electrolytes. I reduced my water intake to one cup a day and increased my exercise, even though my heart was acting up. On Aug. 30, the doctor wanted to talk to me about my vital signs. During this discussion he noticed my hand was turning blue. I was rushed to the infirmary and placed on IV for over two hours. I refused to stay overnight so I was returned back to my cell.

Then on Sept. 3, I stopped drinking water. On Sept. 4, I was rushed to the infirmary and placed on the IV. The plan now was to snatch out the IV, which I did, but during their second attempt to reinsert the IV, the associate warden walked in and informed me that Mr. Dewberry (Sitawa Nantambu Jamaa) was requesting that I attend a phone conference, where he informed me that they – the four main reps – had suspended the hunger strike. Brotha Sitawa told me to tell all the brothas to start re-feeding and end our plans.

The above is pertinent as to my state of mind. I was prepared to sacrifice, so death is my least concern. When I returned back to Pelican Bay on Sept. 10, Brotha Sitawa conveyed to me it is imperative that we report and make public every attempt and/or act of retaliation. Some of us will become priority targets for retaliation, and we must employ every means to expose Pelican Bay and CDCR's repressive tactics toward our peaceful protest.

This is the era of peaceful protests and our methods of operating must complement our peaceful resistance. Me reaching out to the *San Francisco Bay View National Black Newspaper* coincides with this era of peaceful protest.

Years ago, and I'm talking about five years ago, if my captors would have tampered with my food, I would have responded with a weapon in hand and blood in my eyes. But these are methods that have become outdated, and they would only undermine the progress that we have achieved in the past three years. The *Bay View* has been one of the most vital strategic and tactical weapons at our disposal, and we as prisoners of all races are in their debt for life.

Some people have suggested I may be a little paranoid or am overstating the threat (see "'Somebody tried to poison me': Pelican Bay prisoner suspects hunger strike retaliation"). This is why I told Brotha Sitawa I was reluctant to go public. I would rather have my dead body tell the story if it was up to me.

I have spent over 30 years in solitary confinement – isolation – and during this time period I have survived multiple attempts to kill me. For instance, I was placed on an exercise yard with no other New Afrikans, which resulted in two lacerations across my throat, but I survived and subdued my would-be killers. This was just one of many attempts, so if anybody has a right to be paranoid, it's me.

And the potential threats cannot be overstated. Tampering with my food was also a system failure. How did this tampered tray get past the inspection process? Or as Brotha Mutope Duguma suggested: Was this just a practice run to test the inspection process? This time it was ink – next time it could be something more potent. So the question becomes: Do we act now or do we wait until one of us is dead?

Truthfully, Brotha Mutope Duguma months ago warned me and Brotha Sitawa to start inspecting our own food trays. His concerns proved to be valid. We, as New Afrikan political prisoners, agree with the *Bay View's* decision to publish the info on their website. Know that some activists were concerned about liability issues. Allow me to ease your concerns, for I will clearly reiterate my (our) allegation, and that is: My captors tried to poison me and I dare them to challenge my allegations!

George Jackson University – A Statement from its Founder

Within the California Department of Corrections (CDCr), the name George Jackson evokes both fear and hate among prison guards. His very name represents resistance – the epitome of our Black manhood – and this explains in part why the CDCr has spent the last 44 years attempting to censor the name George L. Jackson from within its prisons.

Between 1988 and 2014, no prisoner within the CDCr or any other prison system in this country has suffered more than I for keeping the name George Jackson alive within the Prison Industrial Slave Complex (PISC), and I embrace this suffering without regrets; instead, I wear it as a coat of arms in the service of our revolutionary struggle.

Many within society had suggested at the onset that I (we) change the name of our movement and organization to avoid confrontation with the CDCr/PISC. Even some prisoners have made similar suggestions and explanations to substantiate their position, but I emphatically rejected this suggestion outright.

For unbeknownst to many, the confrontation between the George Jackson University and CDCr was a deliberate and orchestrated strategy. For the past 44 years, since the assassination of Comrade George, the CDCr more than any other fascist, racist government entity within the U.S., has attempted to criminalize and dehumanize Comrade George, reducing him to a gang member, a symbol of prison gang activity – i.e., the Black Guerrilla Family, BGF.

This scheme allowed the CDCr to criminalize any New Afrikan/Black prisoner who dared embrace the legacy and spirit of Comrade George, and this method has worked. Many Brothas are reluctant to even read his books and other writings for fear of being accused of being involved in prison gang activities.

At one time, a false allegation could lead to a life sentence to solitary confinement isolation. I personally spent 32 years in solitary confinement isolation because I refused to abandon Comrade George and all that he had sacrificed in the service of our people!

The question that tends to be at the front of most people's sense of reasoning, why not change the name from the GJU to something else? Why create an unnecessary confrontation? As New Afrikan revolutionaries, we believe that the resolution of contradictions is an imperative component towards facilitating our search for truth, facts and progress.

Comrade George was not a thug or gang member. He was a genuine revolutionary, fighting against the violent state-sponsored racism that was – and still is – prevalent and openly blatant, a reality that the CDCr consistently attempts to divorce from the principles of cause and effect.

Comrade George did not just wake up one morning and decide to make the CDCr our, or his, enemy. Set aside the CDCr's self-serving propaganda and let's look at the facts as they pertain to the oppressive conditions that New Afrikan prisoners were subjected to.

These very conditions are going to require one of two responses: 1) Capitulate to the racist terror that New Afrikan/Black prisoners were being subjected to on a daily basis, or 2) Organize against this blatantly racist state/CDCr-sponsored terrorism and wage a campaign of resistance and self-defense.

Comrade George and others decided to fight back and resist state-sponsored racist-based terrorism, and because of their refusal to capitulate, the CDCr has labeled Comrade George and other New Afrikan revolutionaries of that period, 1967-1978, gang members as a strategic scheme designed to make legitimate resistance illegal and criminal and punish any New Afrikan prisoners who choose the course of legal and legitimate resistance!

This is why it was necessary for me to instigate this open confrontation, to reveal to the people who are the real criminals. This government is no different from Nazi Germany or other fascist regimes that suppress legitimate opposition to their tyranny. Comrade George and other New Afrikan revolutionaries during that time were a direct manifestation of the cause and effect principles: Violent racist oppression is the cause, and New Afrikan resistance is the effect.

So I ask, why should I surrender the truth to appease a lie? I understand that many of you may not support the principles of armed resistance, and I can respect that, but our response at that time was necessitated by the harsh and violent repression that we as New Afrikan prisoners were being subjected to.

No different from the fascist psychosis that is inherent in all fascist regimes, the CDCr was and is offended: How dare you fight us back? Nigger, you should not be resisting.

The CDCr wants us to willingly submit to violent racist oppression. I think not. To abandon the truth as it relates to Comrade George would be equivalent to surrendering to the racism. This truth is not nor has it ever been determined by the very forces responsible for that racist oppression!

We will resist, and the GJU is a testament to our resistance. It is our culture of resistance. Comrade George was one of many who represented our glorious culture of resistance!

If CDCr was all about truth and justice, then help me understand how it openly and passionately supports George Washington, Thomas Jefferson and other presidents and politicians who were openly involved in crimes against humanity. They supported and were willing participants in the system of genocidal slavery.

These leaders also directly participated in a system that is responsible for murdering millions of innocent people, including women and children. CDCr has the audacity to condemn us for supporting the *revolutionary work of Comrade George*, but they have no problem openly supporting white leaders that have the blood of innocent people on their hands, not to mention women and children!

Comrade George was falsely accused of only two murders. George Washington, based on his historical account, is responsible for committing genocide against the Afrikans as well as the indigenous people of North Amerika. We are talking about *millions* of Afrikans that were tortured, raped and murdered in this country under the government-sponsored system of slavery and Jim Crow.

Now you tell me, who is the real criminal, Comrade George or George Washington? If this is about truth and justice, the answer to this question is obvious for anyone seeking the truth. George Washington is the real criminal and gangster.

But if the GJU was GWU, the George Washington University, we would have no problem with the CDCr. In fact, the CDCr would encourage us if not provide us with material support. I should not have to further expound on who is actually fighting the just war as it relates to the GJU and CDCr.

The idea of transforming the New Afrikan criminal mentality did not originate with myself or Dr. Donald R. Evans, who worked with me to found GJU. The original ideas were developed by Comrade W.L. Nolan, George L. Jackson, Howard Tole, John Gordon, Tony Gibson, Death row Jeff, William Christmas, Bunchy Carter, and James Carr, just to name a few.

The idea never had the opportunity to mature due to the CDCr war of violent suppression against New Afrikan prisoners, but our comrades did leave us with a blueprint, and all I did was modify the tactical and strategic application.

Much has changed since the 1960s and early 1970s. What was applicable then is no longer applicable now, so out of necessity I was compelled to modify the idea for GJU but maintain its original objective – the transformation of the New Afrikan criminal mentality. In addition to transforming the New Afrikan mentality, the stabilization of our communities is also one of our primary objectives for GJU.

We have multiple contradictions that are interconnecting. For example, we cannot effectively speak about mass incarceration without speaking about recidivism, nor can we speak about recidivism without effectively speaking about the stabilization of the New Afrikan community, and this is something Comrade George fully understood.

But unfortunately many within the movement had failed to grasp the significance of our approach; the white prison rights activists in particular. So instead of waiting for them to get it, the GJU will chart this course by laying out the most effective blueprint that will be designed to navigate our people and community through the orchestrated government-sponsored scheme designed to facilitate the path from poverty to crime to the prison industrial slave complex (PISC).

The GJU has five primary objectives: 1) To eradicate functional illiteracy among New Afrikan (Black) prisoners. 2) To eradicate cultural ignorance among New Afrikan prisoners. 3) To transform the New Afrikan criminal mentality. 4) To assist in the rebuilding and stabilization of the New Afrikan community. 5) To prepare New Afrikan prisoners for release and reduce New Afrikan recidivism.

People, this is a concrete movement, a movement and organization that is charged with the stabilization of our communities. We cannot effectively resist police brutality from a position of weakness, and our communities are fighting a battle from a position of weakness.

The GJU intends to be at the forefront in transforming the community into a strong, self-reliant and powerful base of operations with the capacity to resist fascism! racism! repression! and oppression!

People, our present goal is to build the necessary formation that is going to get the job done. We are asking for you to join our movement and organization. If you are serious about achieving the above objectives, then we encourage you to join this worthy endeavor.

Before I end this statement, it would be remiss of me not to mention those who have been primarily responsible for keeping the GJU alive and functioning. To be honest, the present success of the GJU is primarily due to their hard work and sacrifices: my Brothas Akili Mwalimu Shakur, Bomani Shakur and Anajaku, just to name a few.

We also encourage people to listen to our radio show, GJU Radio, hosted by Bomani Shakur. Call 347-826-7332 every Wednesday from 5 to 7 p.m. West Coast time and 7 to 9 p.m. East Coast time.

We are presently looking for field coordinators. A field coordinator is responsible for coordinating the GJU in their state or other jurisdiction. Each individual will be screened to avoid enemy infiltration. No law enforcement allowed!

We as a people must get beyond lip service. It's time for action. No one who claims to represent or embrace the spirit of Comrade George can justify just paying lip service. Comrade George was an active soldier and leader; he allowed his actions to reflect what he believes in his heart.

No more talking! We talk too damn much, and then we appear to be at a loss. Why are we still in the positions we are in? Well, I can tell you, too much damn lip service!

I challenge you to challenge us at GJU. Join our organization and movement, and if you're dissatisfied, you can go back to doing whatever the hell you were doing! People, I will now leave you and yours with the gift of profound New Afrikan revolutionary love, trust, respect and support!

Death before dishonor!

ABDUL OLUGBALA SHAKUR

The Haiti Connection: An Open Letter to Black People Everywhere

My beloved people, my name is Abdul Olugbala Shakur, and I am a New Afrikan Freedom Fighter. Born in 1962, I have been active in the service of our people since the early 1970s. I grew up in the struggle. The struggle is my life; it's all I know. I came to prison at the age of 18 for allegedly participating in an armed attack on two white sailors in retaliation for a violent sexual assault on a young sista from the community.

As a realist, I understand I may never step foot beyond this concrete hell again, but I refuse to allow this concrete hell to define who I am or restrain my revolutionary spirit. Though I have spent the past 25 and a half years in solitary confinement – an attempt by my keepers no doubt designed to destroy my spirit – my spirit is free, for I have transcended the concrete hell which contains my physical being.

One of the most pervasive misconceptions pertaining to our imprisoned community is that we lack a sense of humanity or the capacity to empathize, or that we are selfish and always seeking to take advantage of others. This is one of many reasons why society at large tends to allow the prison industrial slave complex to treat us with brutality, as if we are deserving of such inhumane treatment.

I, as a New Afrikan political prisoner of war, know this is not an accurate description of who we are, especially as it relates to New Afrikan political prisoners of war, political prisoners, and politically conscious prisoners and activists. Our good deeds and activist work is often overshadowed by government-sponsored anti-prisoner propaganda.

I believe it is time for us as a collective to display our sense of humanity and come together to save our communities. To exhibit a greater expression of our humanity, let's reach out our hands to help our people in Haiti, to rebuild our international symbol of resistance to global white supremacy and slavery.

Approximately three months ago I received a letter from a young sista inquiring about why I show so much concern for the people of Haiti, especially being that I am not Haitian? I told her I am a New Afrikan and as a New Afrikan I represent the totality of all that is Afrikan – and Afrikan descended – so I embody all that is Black and beautiful.

I am Haitian, I am Jamaican, I am Afro-Cuban, I am Kenyan, I am Afro-Puerto Rican. All that is Afrikan, from Afrika to the rest of the world, their blood also runs through my – our – veins. During the slave trade, the racist slave traders intentionally tried to destroy the Afrikan family – which they believed would facilitate the psychological breaking process.

The slave traders sold family members to different genocidal slave plantations. For example, a mother went to Haiti, her husband to Cuba, her mother to AmeriKKKa, her sista to Brazil, her daughter to the Dominican Republic, and her son to Jamaica. We as a people are descendants of this attempt to execute this global Afrikan genocide, and I refuse to contribute to that genocide by denying my global Afrikan family. As a New Afrikan, I am also Haitian, and I am compelled by this innate affinity to stand up for the rights of our people in Haiti.

I realize that we as a people in this country are faced with our own crises, from the violent deaths of our young people due to gang and drug-related violence and to HIV/AIDS. Our communities are just as unstable as many of the Afrikan-run countries.

Though we can all concede that these unstable conditions have been orchestrated by the forces of white global supremacy, we can't blame racism for our own failure to act in our own best interest. I am not neglecting the problems that we face here in this country. Being part of an imprisoned think tank, the New Afrikan Prisoners Writers' Union, we are equally committed to resolving many of the problems we face as a people.

We have developed a number of proposals designed to address many of the problems we face daily, like gang violence, criminal behavior and the protection of our young women in particular, but the key to our success is coming together as a people and not depending on the government or working with the cops. They don't give a damn about us or our children. We must take the initiative to do for ourselves, and this includes helping our global Afrikan community.

The world became spectators as genocide scourged the sacred Black land of Rwanda. In contrast, when genocide was visited upon the former European nation of Yugoslavia, European nations around the world – AmeriKKKa in particular – mobilized their forces to stop and prevent the genocide of other white people. But they allowed genocide in Afrikan countries to go undeterred. Here we are again being spectators, as genocide ravishes our people in Congo, in Darfur and in Haiti. Yes, Haiti.

What's going on in Haiti is often associated with countries in Afrika, but right here in the Western Hemisphere, a new form of genocide is taking place. Our people in Haiti are faced with conditions that are equal in results to those that exist in Darfur and other places in Afrika, but yet very few people or governments are responding, except to mandate an occupation by United Nations troops, whose main goal is to suppress the People's Revolution for Justice and True Liberation.

My beloved people, it is obvious that we as a people can no longer depend on others to value Black lives. It is quite clear that Black lives do not hold the same human value as white lives in the eyes of European people, which includes white AmeriKKKa. So it is incumbent upon us to move on behalf of protecting, preserving and valuing Black lives, both here and globally.

This task will require direct participation on all our parts, including those of us behind enemy lines. I am particularly appealing to the Black church. In my opinion, the Black church can play one of the most effective roles in intervening in the U.S. government-orchestrated genocide in Haiti. The Black church already possesses the internal infrastructure and capacity to mobilize a grassroots campaign designed to end the genocide in Haiti, and remove the U.S. puppet regime who had gained power via an illegal and unjust coup.

Many have suggested that the Black church is no longer relevant, and an appeal to them would be an act of futility. It is inconceivable to think that the Black church would ignore the plight of our people in Haiti. I refuse to believe this.

The suffering and pain of our people in Haiti have only been exacerbated 10-fold due to the multiple and rapid back to back hurricanes that have hit Haiti. Many people, including children, have died as a direct result of these hurricanes. I, as a New Afrikan freedom fighter, don't expect the forces of global white supremacy to come to the aid of our people in Haiti – no different than the tragedy of Hurricane Katrina.

We as activists knew that our communities were not prepared for a natural disaster. We are now three years removed from Hurricane Katrina, and not one of our communities is prepared for a natural disaster. As soon as another disaster hits, we will be blaming racism again but, I ask, what is stopping us from acting in our own best interest?

When I see the tragedy in Haiti, it is symbolic of our own failure as well. White supremacy nationally or globally is not stronger than the global Black Diaspora, but our strength depends on our ability to come together and *act in our own best interest.*

We have the means and resources at our disposal to improve our living conditions and communities, but our people in Haiti don't have the means, resources or infrastructure to resist global white supremacy and their orchestrated genocide. This is why it is imperative for the global Black Diaspora to respond to their needs and call for help.

We are in a position to serve as an advocate on their behalf. We are in the center of the imperialist monster that is contributing to this genocidal process. We can apply the necessary pressure on this government and their stepchild, the United Nations, to compel them to act in the best interests of the people of Haiti. Though I don't recognize the legitimacy of this fascist government, I believe we have no choice but to attempt to reach them with the hope that they will intervene and end their support for a non-democratic government and demand the immediate release of all political prisoners, POWs and activists.

We as New Afrikan prisoners can help to raise awareness, using the various media, to inform ourselves and educate our communities about the genocidal crisis that has engulfed our beloved Haiti. The more we learn, discuss and write about the crisis in Haiti, the more people will be aware of it.

My beloved people, we hear the cries of suffering that reverberate from the depths of Darfur, Liberia, Congo and all across our Motherland, but we have not heard the cries of suffering and pain from our people in Haiti. I ask: *What have your ears heard to wish to hear no more? And what have your eyes seen to wish to see no more?* Can deafness and blindness be a desired escape from our own reality, with the hope that our problems will go away on their own? Unfortunately, this is not the reality of our situation. It will take a conscious and collective effort to resolve our daily problems.

We are committed to resolving the gang violence in our communities, and we invite you to join our efforts. But we are equally committed to restoring our beloved Haiti. It is important for us to get involved. The lives of many children are at stake and Haiti is not in the position to save their – our – children.

I have spent almost 26 years in solitary confinement – isolation – but I refuse to allow my isolation to serve as an excuse for doing nothing. I am committed to serving *all our people*, especially our babies and children. Seeing the resilience of our beloved Haiti has strengthened my commitment to our global revolutionary liberation struggle – until the last drop of my Black royal blood.

My beloved people, believe me, I understand the reality of the harsh conditions we find ourselves in, and we of the New Afrikan Prisoners Writers' Union are committed to solving the problems we face daily, but we are asking each one of you to make a contribution towards rebuilding our beloved Haiti in the spirit of our beloved generals and liberators Jean-Jacques Dessalines and Toussaint L'Ouverture. We each can contribute something to this worthy cause.

Though the genocide in Darfur embodies the typical elements that define genocide, Haiti is experiencing another form of genocide where the global powers of white supremacy orchestrate conditions that are similar to that of the typical genocide, but make no mistake about it: It is still genocide, and many of our children, women and elders are dying daily.

We can make a difference. Join our struggle to save our beloved Haiti. We must do it for the children. We can no longer turn a deaf ear to their cries of pain. I will now bid you all my love and solidarity! Long live our New Afrikan independence movement!

CHAPTER

SEVEN

JOKA HESHIMA JINSAI

Rationalizing the Irrational: CDCr's Reactionary Defense of its Prison Industrial Slave Complex

83

JOKA HESHIMA JINSAI

Rationalizing the Irrational: CDCr's Reactionary Defense of its Prison Industrial Slave Complex

Greetings, sisters and brothers. The general security policy of CDCr states: "The primary objectives of the Correctional institutions are to protect the public by safely keeping persons committed to the custody of the Secretary of Corrections and Rehabilitation, and to afford such persons with every reasonable opportunity and encouragement to participate in rehabilitative activities." But what happens when state policy runs contrary to the economic and political interests of its employees, administrators and corporate stakeholders?

The recent social progress spearheaded by prisoner human rights activists in long-term solitary confinement which culminated in the Agreement to End Hostilities (AEH) and the abolition of SHU torture policies and served as the catalyst for the passage of such legislative achievements as Proposition 57 has resulted in historically low violence rates on general population facilities, unprecedented positive programming opportunities and participation, drastically reduced recidivism rates and the creation of a culture of rehabilitation among many prisoners where the talk on the yard is about getting out and staying out, as opposed to who and why "it's on."

This trend means the prospect of a significantly smaller prison population in the very near future and, as a result, diminished salaries and job security for CDCr employees. Understand, these seismic shifts in culture were galvanized by California prisoners, NOT CDCr employees or administrators, and this was viewed by CDCr staff and officials as a clear threat to their continued prosperity and job security, a threat to the continued success of their economic model of the Prison Industrial Slave Complex (PISC), a model based on high recidivism, institutional violence, low positive programming opportunities and failed re-entry efforts by prisoners and former prisoners.

Simply put, the high salaries and political influence of the CDCr guards' union, administrators and their corporate partners are dependent on the criminalization and imprisonment of a significant portion of the population in New Afrikan, Latino and poor communities to maintain its appropriation of the social product, i. e., tax dollars and political influence. Prisoners' self-actualized efforts at rehabilitation threaten this.

CDCr employees' interests are threatened by lower violence rates in CDCr general population facilities, increased rehabilitative and reentry rates among offenders and reduced recidivism rates among former prisoners. In plain terms, CDCr's stated aims of safely keeping persons committed to their custody and providing every reasonable opportunity for rehabilitation conflict with the functional aim of the California prison industrial slave complex: to secure lucrative and long-term job security and exorbitant salaries and policy influence in the laws which govern the social lives of citizens across the state.

To combat this threat to their labor aristocracy, CDCr secretary Scott Kernan has announced the absolutely irrational step of implementing "non-designated facilities" across CDCr, which would in effect export reactionary gang violence now isolated on SNY facilities to general population yards across the state – a blatant gambit to plunge general population facilities back into the bad old days of reactionary violence and criminalization.

The rationale of CDCr officials is SNY facilities, in contrast to general population yards, have unprecedented levels of violence and new gangs emerging, while the informants, dropouts, pedophiles and serial rapists which make up such yards and the new gangs on them (gangs which are violently opposed to general population prisoners as the basis of the gangs themselves) would somehow be LESS violent if flooded onto general population facilities among the class of prisoners they were formed to attack. That this is an irrational contradiction is obvious.

For decades, CDCr officials maintained a domestic torture program in SHU facilities at Pelican Bay, Corcoran and Tehachapi state prisons, where, according to the same CDCr officials, "It was necessary to isolate the worst of the worst gang members, those too violent or influential to be housed in the general population, so the remainder of general population prisoners could positively program in peace without the threat of these prison gangs." That many of these prisoners in indeterminate SHU were neither violent nor gang members, particularly in the case of New Afrikan political and politicized prisoners confined to SHU for their ideas alone, was exposed in its abolition. Yet what is relevant here is suddenly CDCr is opting to abandon this precedent in the face of historic success on general population facilities and, in the interest of both reason and public safety, we must ask ourselves why?

Why would CDCr knowingly destabilize the historic progress currently washing across general population yards by flooding them with psychologically unstable EOPs and those who openly advocate their hostility to both general population prisoners and one another, fully conscious such an action will FORCE general population prisoners to defend themselves. Why would they deliberately jeopardize the safety and rehabilitative opportunities of both SNY and general population prisoners when their stated policy is to "safely confine prisoners and provide every reasonable opportunity and encouragement to participate and rehabilitative activities?" Why would you sabotage such historic correctional success, even if it is prisoner led?

The answer is readily available in Secretary Kernan's irrational explanation for the Department's rationale. In both press releases and institutional videos concerning this new non-designated yard policy, CDCr officials have repeatedly made mention of the passage of Proposition 57, prisoner access to milestone completion credits and new opportunities to earn a reduced sentence as part of the catalyst for CDCr officials move to plunge prisons across California into violent conflict.

Frankly, in some of the most warped logic I've heard to date, CDCr official's state: Prisoners released from CDCr custody back to their communities will have to function in society with formerly SNY prisoners, so if they wish to gain access to the opportunities afforded by Proposition 57 and the environment *prisoners* created for its success with the Agreement to End Hostilities, general population prisoners will now have to somehow also function *in prison* with these SNY prisoners these same CDCr officials have deemed the most violent in the state – prisoners responsible for lying on, snitching on or preying on the families of many general population prisoners. As I'm sure any rational and reasonable person has concluded at this juncture, prison, by its very nature, precludes any socialization analogy with free society.

To be sure, following the logic of Mr. Kernan, many of the irrational restrictions in CDCr facilities, most punitive as opposed to safety and security related, should be lifted on prisoners to ensure the prison experience approximates society as closely as possible: Family visitation available to all without exception; no censorship of books, magazines and art references; free access to entrepreneurship and business opportunities for prisoners; open access to text messaging and video chatting for prisoners – *all* reasonable accommodations for the socialization of prisoners while incarcerated, *none* of them likely to materialize anytime soon because CDCr officials are adamantly opposed to them as "contrary to the nature of imprisonment and the confined status of prisoners." Simply put, prison is *not* society.

Prisoners are classified based on multiple factors prior to their placement on a facility to ensure the safety and security of those confined to the custody of CDCr, because conditions in prison are so starkly atypical in comparison to society. Therefore, the notion that this is being done to acclimate general population prisoners to society where SNY designations *don't* exist and you are free to choose your associates and environments is an absurdity bordering on insult.

The truth of the matter is, CDCr employees and administrators are outraged at measures like Proposition 57, SB 261 and prisoner-led initiatives like the Agreement to End Hostilities because they threaten the job security, exorbitant salaries and political influence that CDCr employees have wielded with virtual impunity for the past five decades.

CDCr employees are the highest-paid prison guards in the nation, with a starting salary in excess of $70,000 a year, while the California Correctional Peace Officers Association (CCPOA) remains the most influential lobbying force in the state. With an annual operating budget over $11 billion, corporate and business interests from pharmaceutical firms to agricultural concerns to technology retailers and pay phone providers, they have generated millions of dollars in contracts, all dependent on a robust prisoner population. If current trends in rehabilitation, release and successful reentry to society continue unabated, the need for so many prisons and prison guards to staff them will simply fade away, as will the lucrative contracts to support and supply them.

To counter these legislative efforts and the Agreement to End Hostilities, CDCr plans to introduce a population of prisoners into the general population that general population prisoners will be *forced* to fight: violent SNY gangs. It will ensure a drastic uptick in violent assaults, prosecutions, lost parole dates, lockdowns (where programming opportunities are suspended indefinitely), new sentences for in custody offenses which will translate into robust prisoner population levels, job security and in some instances calls from CDCr for increased budgets to "combat this new wave of violence plaguing the department." A wave of violence designed, orchestrated and implemented by CDCr itself.

Maintaining public safety and ensuring the safe custody of prisoners thus takes a backseat to the maintenance of job security and corporate profits in the largest conflict of interest in U.S. history: We all should be outraged that on the cusp of the success of the most unprecedented prison reform in CDCr history, that CDCr would so deliberately and completely sabotage that success – and play with the lives of tens of thousands of prisoners, their families and communities in the process.

It is incumbent upon us all to voice our outrage at this criminal gambit, no better or less repugnant than the Gladiator Games CDCr staff presided over in Corcoran SHU, only on a much larger and much more lucrative scale. Adverse public opinion is the only sure means of reversing this irrationally sadistic and greed fueled policy.

Contact your representatives, call the Office of Administrative Law and voice your opposition, post on social media and raise awareness of this evil. The collective social progress of our communities and this state hang in the balance. Join Amend the 13th in raising our voices against this evil – and together we can end it.

CHAPTER EIGHT

JOKA HESHIMA JINSAI

A Day in the Life of an Imprisoned Revolutionary

73

JOKA HESHIMA JINSAI

A Day in the Life of an Imprisoned Revolutionary

The purpose of the [Marion] control unit is to control revolutionary attitudes in the prison system and in the society at large.[1]
    – Former Marion Supermax Prison Warden Ralph Aron

In several instances (the control unit) has been used to silence religious leaders. It has been used to silence economic and philosophical dissidents.[2]
    – Federal Judge James Foreman, U.S. District Court,
East St. Louis, Illinois, 1980

...this type of struggle gives us the opportunity to become revolutionaries, the highest form of the human species, and it also allows us to emerge fully as men; those who are unable to achieve either of those two states should say so now and abandon the struggle...[3]
    – Che Guevara, Bolivia, 1967

Greetings, brothers and sisters. Perpetual existence in the sensory deprivation torture units of Amerika, like any form of socio-political violence, is virtually impossible to understand if you've not personally experienced it or some other form of coercive force over a prolonged period. Though the human imagination is infinitely capable of conjuring fantasies of such horrors, what appears equally shocking to many is how can some not only resist such systematic psychological torture, but actually improve themselves under such conditions of extreme duress.

Ironically, the answer lies in the motivation of the torture itself. The origin of our resistance lies in the very nature of the core contradictions of capitalist society in conflict with the advanced elements of its most oppressed strata: the bourgeois state's attempt to stamp out revolutionary sentiment amongst the lumpen-proletariat in hopes of maintaining and expanding its reactionary character, in contrast with the struggle of political and politicized prisoners to raise the consciousness and revolutionary character of the entire underclass, all while resisting the fascist state's attempts to silence our dissent, crush our will to struggle and foment defection.

We have consistently sought to expose the objective reality of our collective exploitation, of what society's ills are, their origins in the arrangement of the productive system, and how to change them in the interests of the vast majority of the world's people. We have consistently been tossed in control units for doing so.

Prison is a socially hostile microcosm of society at large. The same structures and relationships – political, social and economic – that make up U.S. society are reflected on any prison yard, stripped of the pretense of patriotism and unity. Those social forces who dictate society's guidelines – i.e., the ruling class, bourgeois state, the 1 percent etc. – have ensured "the rule of law" is structured to sanction those who would disturb the maintenance of the core contradictions upon which capitalist society is based – i.e., social production leading to private appropriation, the economic class structure, the race caste system etc.

Should critics or dissenters rock the boat too far outside the bourgeois prescribed course, they invariably find themselves ostracized or imprisoned. Once in prison nothing is different. Abuses of imprisoned revolutionaries dates back centuries in the U.S. The legacies of John Brown, Eugene V. Debs, Melvin B. Tolsen, Clifford James, W.L. Nolan and George L. Jackson continue today in the indefinite sensory deprivation isolation of Leonard Peltier, P. Sangu Jones, Mumia Abu Jamal, Sondai Ellis, Zaharibu Dorrough, Sitawa Dewberry, Abdul Olugbala Shakur, D. Mutope Crawford, L. Powell, Wembe Johnson, F.Y. Carter and so many more principled servants of the people and champions of humanity, all daily subjected to indefinite psychological torture solely because they will never renounce the struggle against the oppression of Man and Woman by man and woman … and neither will I. I am a product of this unbroken legacy of revolutionary thought, action and eternal commitment and have shared the same torturous fate for 12 years, and will continue to do so until we win or don't lose, until victory or death.

I've been asked by many human rights activists; "What is it really like, a day in your life?" We share a functional collective consciousness, so sharing a single day from my life should give you a glimpse into the "lives" – the existence – of all these examples of humanity's most noble spirit: the revolutionary in perpetual resistance to indefinite torture.

I wake to darkness and cold. It's 4:30 a.m. and I'm in my small cell in Corcoran SHU (Security Housing Unit). I turn my head slightly to see the photos of my children and grandson on my wall and close my eyes to thank the creator for giving me another day of life in which to make some contribution to the cause of freedom, justice, equality and human rights. I ask that my comrades, my children and my siblings be watched over, their health preserved.

I then open my eyes and rise. It's particularly cold this morning as I lace up my shoes, fold my linen, and roll my mattress back. After attending to my morning ablutions, clean the sink and sweep my floor, I turn on my TV to the news and enjoy a cup of coffee in preparation for my routine.

I have to be extra careful as I change the channel since the last power surge fried my TV cord and if I move my TV it'll blow out again. The c/o (correctional officer) walks past flashing his light into my cell. I have the cell light that glares 24/7 blocked using a piece of string and sheet so I can stave off the migraines that accompany the constant illumination we endure daily.

I watch the various stories engaging bourgeois state-controlled media today: Multinational and domestic corporations, sitting on trillions in cash reserves, are refusing to hire because they claim a combination of "regulatory uncertainty and adverse consumer sentiment" has them sitting on the sidelines of the labor market. I see through this blatant gambit to manipulate the working class into opposing greater financial regulation and health care reform in seconds.

In an economy fueled by consumption, which is directly proportional to wage labor payrolls, corporations are intentionally prolonging the depressed economic cycle by not hiring, thus creating a self-fulfilling prophesy of reduced consumption creating the perception amongst the exploited workers that re-establishing the deregulated free market – which is what caused this current recessionary-recovery cycle – and repealing the petty bourgeois policies of the Obama administration in favor of more industrial bourgeois policies that are championed by Republicans is their only course to broader employment.

I shake my head in a combination of pity, anger and disgust as I hear these deluded patsies parroting the ideas of the ruling class as they languish "trapped in the matrix," their desperate conditions blinding them to their own interests. They continue to grasp and flail ineffectually to realize their immediate interests, seemingly oblivious to any conscious aspirations of changing the system itself, of seizing power and structuring society so the ownership of the means of production and distribution actually reflects the reality of social production and human need.

I immediately berate myself for the direction of my frustrated thought: I remind myself, as I rise and begin my warm-up routine of jumping jacks, that it's not the people's fault when the revolution fails; it is the fault of the vanguard party, our fault … MY fault. I/we must redouble my/our efforts, I think. We must combine our ideas, analyses and efforts in a more effective and efficient form to get our words heard, these ideas understood, these theories tested in the vital arena of social practice.

I did weight work yesterday, filling my laundry bag with stacks of transcripts and old magazines, then lashing them down with pieces of sheet and string to make a weight bag. So today I'll do circuit training. I settle on 10 circuits of five exercises: 50 pushups, 40 crunches, 50 split-lunges, 20 dips (between the bunks) and 50 three-count squats.

The pain in my right side, which has been there since the first hunger strike, is like a piece of shrapnel in my side and by the sixth circuit I'm feeling my age, my body wanting to quit. "No one's here but me," I think. "I'm sweating, I've pushed my body, why continue to endure this pain?" Almost instantly a more insistent voice answers: "What if you were in the field of battle and the lives of your comrades and the people depended on you fighting on? What is pain to the future survival of the people, the party and the revolution? Nothing at all." All life is suffering; it is the nature of your existence, the price of your unwavering commitment to what is right.

I heed this second voice. I ignore the pain and exhaustion and push on. I feel the cold stone under my palms and the sweat flowing from my pores, but none of it registers in my mind. I am fueled by images of combating the sick bastards on this TV who are dragging an old woman away in cuffs, her head bloodied, from an Occupy Movement protest line.

I strive to control the fire, to channel it into my exercises, and just as the rage against all the injustice I've witnessed and endured at the hands of this sick system seeks to overwhelm my reason, my discipline clamps down on it, I detach from my emotions, and finish my last set. I pace my small cell and drink a cup of warm water, reasserting greater control of my breathing and heart rate in preparation for the next half of my morning regimen, cataloguing the work I have before me today and prioritizing it.

The c/o's walk by for morning count and unlock the barbox – the sound of the metal gears falling into place, of tray slots being unlocked in preparation for chow signaling the start of another day in the torture unit. When they leave the section, I put up my window blockers and do 45 minutes to an hour of kata and martial arts training.

Here in the 4B1L-C section short corridor, the windows in the gun tower are mirror-tinted and the section windows blacked out. They can watch you, but if they're staging a raid or monitoring your in-cell activities, you can't see them. You thus live in a state between perpetual uncertainty and hyper-vigilance, never knowing when you'll have your cell torn up and property destroyed or confiscated.

They are aware most imprisoned New Afrikan revolutionary nationalists practice some form of self-defense, and they believe they have sufficient documentation as to the extent of my decades of attention to these sciences in my C-file and elsewhere, but they really don't, so I prefer to train in conditions of privacy to keep the extent of my expertise to myself. I end with some light moving meditation and then take my bird bath.

Around this time they are coming through the section door with chow. It's scrambled eggs and potatoes today; it's Tuesday. The menu never changes. You know the meal by the day of the week. We're being served on paper trays, the food is grossly under-proportioned and ice cold. I go to the door and accept my small tray of food and sack lunch, looking at these c/o's laugh and joke about the game they enjoyed over the weekend.

Through hooded eyes, I speak politely, thanking them for the cold food and wishing them a good morning. Startled by this response, they offer a nervous pleasantry in reply. I deposit my meal in a white paper cup, place the 2 slices of bread over it and scoop the

3-½ spoonful's of cold cracked wheat cereal into my mouth and wash them down with some warm water.

I see this for the subtle psychological attack it is, reminding myself provocation and/or mental degradation is its intent. I form the opposite reaction, remembering there are men and women right now in some CIA black site prison in Uzbekistan being raped with a cattle-prod for breakfast yet maintaining their ideological integrity. I'll do no less. The fact that they've been feeding me this way for 12 years and counting only strengthens my resolve. I'm desensitized by this point. I eat only to survive. I stopped eating for taste, texture or temperature years ago.

I finish my "bird bath," clean my sink, toilet, walls and floor, then sit down and eat half of my eggs and potatoes, saving the rest to eat with my lunch. My sack lunch – one slice of bread, two thin slices of bologna, a pack of two graham crackers and a small pack of almonds (12 almonds in a pack) – needs these extra calories to hold me till chow at 5 p.m. I make my coffee pack, sit down and open my "office." I intentionally maintain a massive workload so all of my time is consumed with activity. I am very conscious of time, of the quantity and quality of my daily service to the revolutionary cause.

I'm doing a portrait of a family who's befriended my comrade Kambui in hopes of strengthening those social ties and displaying the quality of my/our work to a broader public audience; I'm designing new pieces for my/our greeting card line in hopes of raising funds for our progressive community development programs; I'm litigating a medical civil rights claim on behalf of a prisoner here with diabetes where I've been forced to file four different motions for extension of time because we've not been given law library access since August.

We're supposed to get law library access today. I have several chapters and papers I have to review in various texts on economics, politics and mass psychology for a new piece we're writing on the practical application of Revolutionary Scientific Socialism in the U.S. today. I'm helping some good comrades gain a broader understanding of the ideas of Fanon, Marx, Engels, Mao, Trotsky and Ho Chi Minh as they relate to the ever-evolving conditions in modern society, trying to finish some work for our brothers and sisters in the progressive media and the Occupy Movement and putting the finishing touches on a Japanese cultural piece I/we initially intended to donate to the Fresno Museum of Art to auction off for the Japanese Tsunami Relief Fund but can only assume the museum director never wrote back because we are prisoners and she could not see past the propaganda of the state and its corresponding social stigma.

I take on all these projects, and more, intentionally. Enforced idleness is a key element of the sensory deprivation torture unit. The isolation is designed to concentrate the psychological impact of this endless idleness. The mind is supposed to turn in upon itself, warping reality. It is structured to reinforce the concept that you have nothing to look forward to but the same nothing ... forever. Its purpose is to break the minds of weak men, to transform them into craven informants, agents of the state, rats, de-briefers.

The mind of the developed and committed revolutionary cannot be broken. Whenever it encounters such adverse conditions, it changes those conditions. I/we have no "idle time." From the lowest, most oppressive conditions in this society, the SHU, we struggle daily to advance the progress of humanity itself.

We must work ten times harder than any other segment of society to have the most miniscule influence on human affairs because we have such overwhelming power arrayed against us with the sole purpose of repressing our ideas – i.e., IGI (Institutional Gang Investigations), ISU (Investigations Services Unit), prison administrators, state officials, the U.S. federal government, decades of false propaganda and entrenched social stigmas which have created an aversion and irrational skepticism of anything positive and progressive originating here.

We have a monumental task just overcoming the obstacles to communicate with you all. We have far too much work to do by writ of our chosen lifestyle to ever fall prey to such an innovation in psychological coercion. We are not simply immune, but where the truly committed are concerned, such attempts have the opposite effect: The fact that they would even attempt such attacks on dedicated servants of the people only hardens our resolve to resist. It makes us more revolutionary, better servants of the people and better men.

So I sit here for the first half of my day and work on this portrait. As I work, my thoughts tend to drift to my regrets. I've been imprisoned for most of my children's lives and thoughts of their welfare and safety consume me: What are their interests and views, what do they value, what do they love? I look at the photo of my daughter Jawanda. I've never seen her face in real life or heard her laughter. I write them all (I have five children) at least once a month or more, but it's been years since I've heard from most of them. I'm convinced my daughter Jawanda hates me for not being there for her and her brother as they grew up.

I push the thoughts away, comforted in the knowledge that my daily efforts in the cause are the greatest gift I could give them: a world where the interests of the many actually govern its direction and nature, democracy in form and not simply in word. Though I will not live to see the victorious revolutionary change for which I have labored all their lives, and will continue to for the remainder of my own, their children just might usher in this new social order on the heels of our contributions.

I hear keys as the section door opens and IGI officers enter the section wearing their arrogance and warped perceptions literally on their sleeves. They're here to escort someone to ACH (hospital clinic). As they do so, the nurse and escort officer walk the tier dispensing medication. I accept and take my own meds, treatment for the inescapable damage done to my own mind which has manifested itself in an actual imbalance in my brain chemistry. I ask the officer, "Are they going to run law library?" They haven't called with a list yet. But "doubt it," he says.

I leave the door and return to my work, suppressing the sharp spike of anger at their continued refusal to allow us to access the courts to redress these inhumane violations of our rights. Another log on the pyre of the daily usurpations of our basic rights. Before I know it, it's noon and I set my artwork aside and prepare my lunch while the news plays in the background.

I pick up the book Zaharibu sent down to me, *New Theories of Revolution* by Jack Woddis, and I pick up where I left off as I finish my meal. Most of the texts and concepts Brother Woddis is critiquing are close at hand and by the time my meal is finished and sufficiently digested, I have several tomes opened, cross-referencing ideas and concepts while I simultaneously view them through the prism of current social conditions and my own dialectical analysis.

I save two slices of bread, my apple and a slice of bologna from my lunch so I'll have something to look forward to this evening. With that done, I turn my attention to addressing a question one of my comrades had on whether the practice of several small businesses trading among themselves to keep their overheads low equated a form of socialism, having seen the same story on PBS. I explained to the comrade his question underscores the importance of ideological development and a firm grasp of historical materialism when analyzing socio-economic phenomena.

What he had observed was a barter system amongst petty-bourgeois proprietors in an intra-class conflict with the more powerful industrial bourgeois interest – in this case Wal-Mart; this was not socialism. Those small businesses continue to offer their goods and services to consumers at a profit mark-up, continue to appropriate the surplus value of their workers' labor, continue to support this system of white male privilege, race-class divide and rule, and labor exploitation. They are not socialist or revolutionary; quite the opposite, they are reactionary as they seek to turn back the wheel of history to the point where their mode of small production was the dominant segment of the bourgeois class base, where now they seek to band together against the ruling bourgeois strata to keep from being cast back down into the working class because they can't compete with the ruling bourgeois' industrial scale mode of production and labor exploitation.

Socialism does not seek to "reform" capitalist property relations amongst the bourgeois elements; no, socialism seeks to abolish bourgeois property relations altogether. I went in depth on the question as did other comrades. Mind you, because we are in a sensory deprivation torture unit, these discussions cannot be held verbally, no. We must write them on paper, then shoot our lines and "fish" them to and fro amongst each other, sharing ideas, lending moral, emotional, psychological, material and spiritual support to one another via a piece of string and a weighted item tossed down the tier from one cell to another.

Because of blockers welded to the base of the doors and c/o's who will snatch and break your line, this is of course difficult. But again none will deter us from exercising our fundamental human rights. We are here only because we believe the oppression of Man and Woman by man and woman should be opposed.

By the time I finish, evening chow has come. I set my cake aside as a special treat for later and watch Nightly Business Report as I finish my meal, assessing and analyzing the daily permutations of global capitalism; then I watch BBC News and PBS News hour. I then get back in "the office" and work on political pieces for various media interests, until I run out of gas around 8 p.m.

But I have one more thing to do. Today is special to me, and as I've done for the past 17 years of my imprisonment – this is now my 18th – I write a letter to my son giving him the benefit of my life's experiences for the year, summing it up by recounting a story of children in India who are sent in bulk by labor firms to plantation factories as young as 9, 10 and 11 to pick cotton and work the gins in conditions as deplorable as those we experienced in the chattel slave epoch to develop textiles for a mega-rich British multinational. I explain to him that this was evil and how all that was necessary for such evil to continually prevail was for good people to do nothing.

I end my letter, slide it into the tray slot and sit down to enjoy a comedy program on TV while I eat the items I've saved from my earlier meals. Conscious of the pain in my side and health benefits of laughter, both chemically and psychologically, I release my emotional control and allow myself again to feel. I let go of the melancholy which is my constant companion and allow the mirth to strike me in the belly as the underclass antics of Raising Hope play across my TV.

I hear the section door pop, the bar box being opened and the gears being locked back in place as the other c/o passes out mail. It's a special day; I'm expecting some mail and hoping to hear from my son. I receive a card wishing me holiday greetings from the beautiful brothers and sisters from a Pasadena community parish in solidarity with the prisoner hunger strike coalition. It fills me with gratitude and warmth. Its 29 days old and postmarked, meaning IGI held this meager card for at least 26 days. I also get a ducat for blood draw in the morning.

I leave my door and laugh away the disappointment of not hearing from my family on this day, as I enjoy the 10 o'clock news. I see a wonderful story in honor of Muhammad Ali's birthday, on how he defied the U.S. war machine by refusing to submit to coercion into their imperialist adventure in Vietnam. I suddenly feel even better, knowing I'm in such good company.

I look at my children's photos and the images of Chairman Mao, Bob Marley, Jonathan Jackson and Buddha that are the only other images on my wall. I again close my eyes and ask the creator to watch over and bless my comrades, my children, my siblings, parents and all the people languishing under the yoke of this global Moloch of greed we call the capitalist "free market." I close my eyes wondering why I heard from no one. I cut off my TV. I have an early start in the morning. I'm not as young as I used to be. Today was my birthday: Jan. 17, 2012.

Our existence here is one of struggle, of constant, ever present, inescapable daily struggle. I/we have attempted to convey this reality to you in many ways, but these are words, only valid if they serve to influence you positively in some way. What must be understood in the final analysis is we here are not "gang members" when speaking of adherents of NARN (New Afrikan Revolutionary Nation/Scientific Socialism; we are revolutionaries. We think, act and communicate differently than those who have not given their lives to the people.

I say this not to disparage anyone; it is simply a statement of fact. The Honorable Comrade George Lester Jackson stated, "Revolution is a war for the minds of the masses." The state has buried us in these torture units specifically to ensure we cannot effectively communicate the reality of the collective subjugation of 99 percent of those in this society to the whims of an avaricious ruling elite. They seek to criminalize legitimate political discourse, to disparage the truth in favor of an ever-evolving lie. The truth of the matter is you and I both are nothing but commodities to these people, our values being exploited or intentionally suppressed as the interests of their profit margins dictate.

Saul D. Alinsky in his book *Rules for Radicals* said, "When you are trying to communicate and can't find the point in the experience of the other party at which he can receive and understand, then you must create the experience for him."[4] I have tried to do that here without horrifying you. What must be understood is some of the greatest political, social, economic, cultural, scientific and military minds of our time are languishing in the short corridors and cell blocks of Pelican Bay and Corcoran SHUs. Many of you in progressive circles are familiar with my writing, but I am merely a product of the phenomenal principled men I mentioned at the beginning of this discussion and the unfinished legacy of democratic change and equalitarian struggle that is the hallmark of the evolution of civilization.

Under these conditions – indeterminate SHU confinement – we have the full weight of the state arrayed against us. Our words in some instances are our only effective tools. If I/we write or say something I/we consider revolutionary, that I hope will alter the nature and structure of society and improve mankind, but in the final analysis fails to move anyone in a substantive way, it is not revolutionary or progressive. Communication that fails to affect its intent is so much idle chatter.

The concrete analysis of such concrete conditions would be nothing has been changed. The reason we commit so much time and effort into understanding the history and present interconnections of all human activity in our world is the ability to change people's minds, to alter their perspectives so a previously hidden truth becomes self-evident. It's a serious matter, as serious and strategic as war, because revolution is a war.

As you read this I'm waging that war now, against entrenched biases and artificial social stigmas manufactured by a specific socio-economic interest. This is why we are so hard on ourselves, why we intentionally expose ourselves to conditions that would crush most men's minds and subsume their wills: Failure to communicate these ideas to you effectively is to fail you.

We are speaking of the future evolution of the world, of forging a society more reflective of human decency than human misery. We cannot fail. Our cause is just because our cause is you – serving the people.

It is my sincerest hope that you leave this brief discussion with not simply a greater grasp of this injustice, but more centrally with a determination to insist the state end this hidden hypocrisy. The U.S. – and the state of California – cannot continue criticizing Syria, China, Burma and Russia for their alleged repressive measures against dissent and maltreatment of political prisoners, yet continue to maintain its own domestic program of torture against political prisoners. It is inhumane, illegal, hypocritical and just plain wrong.

Our imprisonment has no bearing on the truth and validity of our ideas. If this is truly a nation which values democracy, equality, human rights and fundamental fairness as its social imperatives, surely its people cannot allow this practice of political repression to continue unchallenged. Surely you will challenge it.

If nothing else, I hope sharing a day in my life will compel you to value your own a little more and cherish that of your fellow man or woman as you do your own. My/our love, loyalty and solidarity to you all … until we win or don't lose.

CHAPTER NINE

JOKA HESHIMA JINSAI

∿∿∿∿∿∿∿∿∿∿∿

Amend the 13th: Abolish Legal Slavery in Amerika
Movement Mission Statement
106

JOKA HESHIMA JINSAI

Amend the 13th: Abolish Legal Slavery in Amerika Movement Mission Statement

Preamble

Section One of the 13th Amendment outlawed slavery and involuntary servitude "except as punishment for crime whereof the party shall have been duly convicted"... Such an amendment amounted to an escape clause, a corrective loophole that left a form of slavery intact ... In the very sentence abolishing slavery, provision had been made for its revival under another form and through the action of the U.S. courts. The 13th Amendment marked the discursive link between the civilly dead felon and the slave or social non person ... This amendment is essential to understanding how the burdens and disabilities that constituted the badges of slavery took powerful hold on the language of penal compulsion. Once the connection to prison and slaves had been made, slavery could resurface under other names, not only in the South but also in the North.[1]

– Colin Dayan

*A*merika is a slave state – a nation whose wealth and prestige rest upon the subjugation and exploitation of other humans. The rationalization for slavery of any sort requires the enslaver(s) to dehumanize the subjects of their domination, to deny or unmake their personhood as a legitimate expression of their idea of civilization.

Dialectically, to a great extent, it also requires the enslaved to accept their dehumanization. In Amerika this process of transmuting people from humans into slaves is carried out through the "rule of law." Slavery is legal in the United States. I don't mean it was legal, but it IS legal and has always, in one form or another, been a cornerstone of the hierarchical structure of Amerikan society.

That slavery remains legal in the U.S., though disturbing, is not as shocking as the fact the vast majority of U.S. citizens don't know slavery remains "legal." Perhaps the primary reason for this willful ignorance lies in the process by which the social stigma the U.S. attaches to slaves has been transferred to those convicted of a felony.

The same rationale which governed the ruling class and states perspective on the New Afrikan, Native and, to a lesser extent, Latinos and the poor prior to the "Emancipation Proclamation" governed it afterwards. In fashioning the basis for this next phase of "legal" oppression, the ruling class and its state, with Machiavellian calculation, embedded a pretext in which to preserve slavery in the very language of the constitutional amendment to abolish it. The 13th Amendment to the Constitution, the "supreme law of the land," states: "Neither slavery nor involuntary servitude, except as punishment for a crime whereof the party shall have been duly convicted, shall exist within the United States." Because the ruling class and the state controlled – and in many cases was – the productive system and the judicial machinery of society, manufacturing "laws" and socio-economic conditions which constantly exposed a particular population to criminal conviction or stigmatization based on those "laws" was as simple as flipping a switch on the assembly lines of their factories.

From 1862 to the present day, Amerikan criminology and legislative effect would be a series of refinements on this single theme: the systematic criminalization of New Afrikans (Blacks), other oppressed nationalities and the poor – populations designated for exploitation or disposal by the U.S. from its inception.

Political opposition to the legal slavery provision of the 13th Amendment is not new among NARN adherents. Comrade George, Comrade Khatari, Comrade Jalil Muntaquin and many others have called for its abolition and organized toward that end, but none have yet to succeed in forging a structure and national movement solely dedicated to abolishing legal slavery in Amerika and all the unequal social, political and economic relationships enforced by its attendant statutes.

Development of the concept and strategy for the "Amend the 13th: Abolish legal slavery in Amerika movement" began in November 2013 following the close of the third hunger strike here in California, after holding discussions and issuing statements with other think tank coordinators on the next logical step for our anti-prison industrial slave complex (PISC) struggle. Since that time, the centrality of the slavery provision of the 13th Amendment has gained a degree of social resonance with many, like Comrade Malik in Texas and "Free" movements, including the Free Alabama Movement, IWOC, New Underground Railroad etc., across the South, sounding the call to abolish "legal" slavery in Amerika.

The primary rationale for "Amend the 13th" is simple: There are thousands of dynamic progressive groups and activists engaging the system in disparate aspects of anti-PISC work, in effect waging the same struggle at many different points. Yet this beast is so big, so powerful, so ingrained in Amerikan social life that – outside of mass social cooperation like that seen in the 2011- 2013 California Hunger Strikes – it is able to ignore, absorb or superficially reform away our individual attacks, while keeping the heart of all these contradictions protected under layers of constitutional legitimacy and conditioned public support.

The heart of these contradictions – no matter what we, our organizations or communities are fighting against – is the slavery provision of the 13th Amendment. "Amend the 13th" seeks to unite and concentrate all our organizations and mobilize power to strike at this single point of "legal" hate and oppression – repeatedly – while simultaneously ensuring each of us can continue to pursue our own individual social progress missions, until the very basis of legal slavery is abolished completely.

This means striking at the nexus of its oppressive rationale: that slavery under any circumstance (even as a punishment for crime) is legal and legitimate under U.S. law is fundamentally incorrect. Such a rationalization can only exist with the acceptance and participation of the Amerikan people. *Your* acceptance and participation in slavery.

WHY "AMEND THE 13TH" IS NECESSARY

The maintenance of slavery in the U.S. and its constant evolution is designed to maintain both the physical structures of race and class oppression and the psychological and ideological character structures upon which the capitalist system is based. What we must understand is the modern slavery enforced by the 13th Amendment is merely a single cog in a global network of oppressive and exploitative relationships.

These exploitative social relationships manifest themselves not only in the enslavement and commoditization of those convicted of a crime, but also in the pseudo-enslavement of immigrants on rural farms and domestic workers forced to accept low wages and/or sexual harassment from employers for fear of deportation; they manifest themselves in the enslavement of women and children forced into the sex slave trade or domestic roles by pimps and traffickers in communities across Amerika; they manifest themselves in the involuntary or compulsory servitude of children in India, Liberia, Thailand, Congo, Bangladesh and elsewhere forced to work in sweatshop factories and mines for Amerikan corporations or interests.

When we look upon these horrors, we tend to view them in their isolation as opposed to their interconnection. In doing so, we fail to see these systems of exploitation are all in fact contiguous parts of the U.S. socioeconomic infrastructure. Hierarchical authoritarian systems, like U.S. capitalism, cannot function without these populations forced to the bottom rung of society acting as surplus labor or human chattel. Neither can they function without the complicity of broad sections of the population in such dehumanization.

Sexism and xenophobia play just as crucial a role in the social divisions of the capitalist arrangement as do racism and classism. These systems of exploitation and hate are institutional and self-perpetuating in Amerika – so deeply rooted in the core psychology of so many of us that a corresponding systematic approach will be required to dismantle them.

Before there can be any serious talk of degrading the social foundations of supremacy and hate, we must eliminate their embodiment in "law." Slavery and involuntary servitude for anyone – even those convicted of a crime – is itself criminal, morally repugnant and indefensible.

The United States – to my knowledge – is the only nation on the planet Earth which maintains a "legal" provision by which its own citizens can be reduced to "slaves of the state" within its national Constitution. Surely we cannot allow such hypocrisy to continue striding the world stage, declaring itself the bastion of "freedom and democracy."

But this is only half the reason "Amend the 13th" is so necessary. There is also the question of "civil death," which, in spite of popular belief, extends the slavery provision of the 13th Amendment far beyond the prison walls. Today modern slavery is erected in "civil death" laws and social containment policies for most anyone convicted of a felony at some point in their lives.

"Civil death" laws successfully unmake the personhood of people and convey the social stigmatization of the chattel slave onto the criminal offender, divorcing them from humanity and the compassion humans commonly show their fellow man/woman. "Civil death" laws deliberately and disproportionately impact New Afrikans, Latinos and the poor, exacerbating centuries of poverty, social containment and desperate human misery – the perfect conditions for the development of the underground economy upon which imprisonment is based.

This is not by chance or happenstance, but by design. A cursory glimpse at just a few "civil death" laws reveals their intent to maximize poverty and recidivism among those subject to them: In many states, former prisoners have restrictions on driving thus making, looking for, or maintaining a job very difficult. Those convicted of a felony in the U.S. are automatically banned from holding certain professional licenses, such as barber or accountant.

In California alone there are over 212 "laws" preventing ex-offenders from getting certain jobs or professional licenses, and there are similar statutes across the U.S. at the state and federal level. This constitutes the deliberate application of poverty and recidivism. According to the U.S. Bureau of Justice Statistics 2013-2014, 87 percent of all criminal offenders live near or below the poverty line.

Prisoners cannot own or operate a business under U.S. law. This is wholly irrational. If it is the contention of the state that a debt to society is owed as a consequence of violating their "law," why would anyone erect laws which bar them from making a contribution to the economy and labor market if they possess the business acumen to do so? You wouldn't unless your intent was to deliberately impose poverty and dependence on those subject to your control.

Slaves under U.S. "law" are "non-persons," and thus cannot vote. Disenfranchisement "laws" have crippled the electorate in New Afrikan and poor communities. One in three New Afrikans cannot vote due to a felony conviction, and 1.4 million of them are New Afrikan males. These communities are subject to laws they have little to no influence over, such as "gang injunctions" and "stop and frisk" statutes, because so many are removed from the process by which "laws" are made or opposed. The combined impact of these, and many other "civil death" laws is to reduce those subject to them to a subhuman state; a social, economic and political position outside and beneath that of others in this nation.

To be a slave in modern Amerika is a study in limited options, codified stigmatization and the absolute despotism of the state in every aspect of social life. This continued legitimization of slavery in any form, for any population, is to enforce social alienation on that population so severe that the state often produces the very anti-social attitudes and actions the "law" is supposed to be intended to remedy.

Abolition of the slavery provision of the 13th Amendment would re-actualize the personhood of those who have had their very humanity stripped from them and in so doing create a vested interest in the former slave to participate in the progress of their communities. As such, the scope of "Amend the 13th" will encompass the development of autonomous institutions which will empower the communities of former slaves socially, politically, and economically – which is in the interests of society as a whole.

MOVEMENT STRATEGY AND STRUCTURE

The "Amend the 13th: Abolish "Legal" Slavery in Amerika Movement" is an all-inclusive, coalition-based national campaign and community-based organizing effort which is determined to remove the "legal" and social basis for the dehumanization of those subject to the judicial machinery of the United States – and finally abolish slavery in Amerika once and for all. The movement has three basic aims:

To amend the 13th Amendment to the U.S. Constitution to remove its "legal" slavery provision for all persons: including those found guilty and sentenced for a felony offence.

1. To abolish and/or repeal all "civil death" and social containment statutes and ordinances which do not afford prisoners, ex-offenders and their communities full human, political, economic and participatory rights in social life in Amerika that derive their power from the 13th Amendment.

2. To develop and implement as quickly as possible autonomous community-based economic, political and social infrastructure capable of eliminating, mitigating or diminishing to the greatest degree the negative impact of mass incarceration, criminalization and "legal" slavery on our communities [i.e. Autonomous Infrastructure Mission (A.I.M.)].

We will seek to accomplish this end via a three-pronged strategy designed to raise social awareness of and public opposition to the continuation of "legal" slavery in Amerika, while simultaneously undermining its basis.

1. Organize a national petition drive to amend the 13th Amendment to remove its "legal" slavery provision at the federal level, and a corresponding petition in each state to rescind all "civil death" and social containment "laws" which derive their powers from the "legal" slavery provision of the 13th Amendment.

2. Carry out targeted demonstrations which highlight both the negative social impact and continued existence of "legal" slavery in Amerika.

3. Promote and seek formal authority for the implementation of community-based parole, pardon and clemency review boards based on the concept of "Strategic Release."

The structure of "Amend the 13th," in keeping with its aim to forge a national coalition inclusive of every group, activist and individual opposed to "legal" slavery in Amerika in all its guises (i.e., criminalization, mass incarceration, disenfranchisement, "civil death," involuntary servitude, the deliberate applications of poverty, etc.) will seek State Coordinators from already existing organizations and/or activists in each state.

These State Coordinators will be responsible for creating their own state coordinating committees reflective of the activists, organizations and affected communities in their state. They will also be responsible for recruiting City Coordinators to conduct signature drives, organize community participation in development and stability initiatives, organize demonstrations, garner support for community-based parole, pardon and clemency boards – and "strategic release" – and expand political and material support for the movement nationally.

Each state coordinator will coordinate their efforts with the "Amend The 13th" national coordinating committee, which will include founder Joka Heshima Jinsai and an Executive Director, Deputy Director, Chief Inside Coordinator, Deputy Inside Coordinator, Secretary, National Treasurer, Community Development Coordinator, National Spokesperson and Executive Legal Consultant.

The primary function of the National Coordinating Committee is to see that the three basic aims of "Amend the 13th" are realized via its three-pronged strategy, and ensure sufficient human and material resources are available to state and city coordinators to realize these goals. Building a successful movement begins with developing a competent and effective structure capable of being the living counterpoint to the existence of the prison industrial slave complex.

We understand conditions and points of resistance differ from state to state. The struggles being waged in Georgia and Alabama in the 2010s were successfully waged in California and New York in the 1970s. However, what is constant across every state is the "legal" and political basis for all the various forms of abuse, exploitation and dehumanization experienced by those subject to the judicial machinery in the U.S.: the "civil death" and slavery provisions of the 13th Amendment. Striking at these as one will undermine the entire dehumanization rationale of U.S. penal policy and jurisprudence which stems from the conscious preservation of the slave system in its modern, punitive form. Social attitudes flow from social conditions, and social conditions are influenced by social attitudes; as such, the minds of the people – your minds – are the primary battleground for social progress.

The unfortunate truth is that most U.S. educational institutions teach *what* to think, and rarely *how* to think. "Amend the 13th" seeks to provide the people with an opportunity to not only explore critical thought, but to also confront the hate which continues to cast a pall over social relationships at every level of Amerikan society. It allows us to not simply alter the basis for inhumane "laws" and codified hate, but to also alter the institutions and social life in the most desperate and besieged communities in such a way that it strikes at the very origins of crime, criminalization and human misery.

If we can agree the disproportionate distribution of wealth, privilege, access and opportunity in a society is the origin of all crime and the gateway to enslavement in the U.S., then the most prudent course is to invoke its opposite – to create independent wealth, access and opportunity in those communities which enjoy so little of it. Stable and prosperous communities produce stable and prosperous people. Therefore, "Amend the 13th's" intent is to empower the modern slave socially, politically and economically in the social interests of society as a whole; conversely, opposition to it would run contrary to those interests.

In the final analysis, the complete abolition of slavery in the United States is a historical imperative. It is our responsibility as principled people to finally end this willful hate, this intentional social containment and the tissue-thin façade that it is not willful and intentional. The U.S. state must be held accountable by the people – and the world – for preserving the vilest practice in the history of civilization in the body of "the supreme law of the land."

When we speak of fascism in Amerika, we are speaking of the maintenance of authoritarian ideology, the perpetuation of hate, under the guise of "national security, national interests and patriotism." U.S.

pronouncements of "freedom and justice for all" in the face of "legal" slavery is not mere political hypocrisy, but an ideal manifestation of the rationalization of fascism, and we must reject it, oppose it and overcome it.

We must all recognize that any social force which opposes this movement's goals are forces which support the maintenance of slavery in Amerika. They must be exposed as such. Our social cooperation and unity of purpose at this critical juncture in history are capable of accomplishing what should have been realized over 100 years ago: The abolition of legal slavery in Amerika.

If you believe us correct in this lofty goal, join us, build with us, demand and enforce through our collective action a society free of institutional hate and oppression – and build it. We look forward to building with you all toward this historic change.

Until we win or don't lose.

CHAPTER

TEN

JOKA HESHIMA JINSAI

∿∿∿∿∿∿∿∿∿∿

On Self-Defense Against Racist Murder

118

JOKA HESHIMA JINSAI

On Self-Defense Against Racist Murder

Part 1
It is well known that the Black race is the most oppressed
and most exploited of the human family. It is well known
that the spread of capitalism and the discovery of the New
World had as an immediate result the rebirth of slavery,
which was for centuries ... a bitter disgrace on mankind.
What everyone does not perhaps know is that after ...
years of so called "emancipation," American Negroes still
endure atrocious moral and material suffering, of which the
most cruel and horrible is the custom of lynching ...
Imagine a furious horde, fists clenched, eyes bloodshot,
mouths foaming, yells, insults, curses ... They are armed
with sticks, torches, revolvers, ropes, knives, scissors,
vitriol, daggers – in a word, with all that can be used to kill
or wound ... In a wave of hatred and bestiality, the
lynchers drag the Black to ... a public place ... When
everyone has had enough, the corpse is brought down ...
While on the ground stinking of fat and smoke, a black
head, mutilated, roasted, deformed, grins horribly and
seems to ask the setting sun, 'Is this civilization?'[1]

— Chairman Ho Chi Minh, 1924

Instead of trying to avoid conflict or whining about the injustice of it all, consider an option developed over the centuries by … strategists to deal with violent and acquisitive neighbors; reverse intimidation. The art of deterrence rests on three basic facts about war and human nature: First, people are more likely to attack you if they see you are weak and vulnerable; second, they depend on the signs you give out, through your behavior both past and present; third, they are after easy victories, quick and bloodless. That is why they prey on the vulnerable and weak.[2]

— Robert Greene

The need to not mistake enemies for friends is especially great for us. Part of the reason for us being issue oriented is that we don't yet see the need to assume responsibility in the development of the strategies affecting our lives. Those who are misgoverned and oppressed merely respond to the oppressive issues and conditions as they arise, and as the suffering triggers our awareness.[3]

— James Yaki Sayles

For two or more centuries, America has marched proudly in the van of human hatred — making bonfires of human flesh and laughing at them hideously, and making the insulting of millions more than a matter of dislike — rather, a great religion, a world war-cry.[4]

— W.E.B. DuBois

Greetings, Sisters and Brothers. Amerikkka is a sick state — its social ills the product of the malignant sickness of ruling class morality. For us to make sense of the relentless, 400-year-long onslaught of racist violence against New Afrikans and other nationally oppressed people in Amerika and the absence of a collective program of comprehensive self-defense and secure communities among the majority of the New Afrikan population in the U.S., it's important we first grasp the origin of this contradiction, as all other points of contradiction and irrationality flow from it.

There is a direct correlation between the origin of U.S. society, the relationship of New Afrikans in its development, the racist murder of nine women, men and youth in Emanuel A.M.E. Church, the ongoing wave of Euro-Amerikan police slaughtering New Afrikans in their communities, and our failure to develop a national policy of self-defense. To understand that correlation, we must trace its etiology.

The mode of production and appropriation is what determines the composition of a society and which class will rule it. When the Euro-Amerikan bourgeois settlers overthrew colonial British socio-economic organization in North Amerika, it retained for itself the same privileges of usurpation that the aristocracy had so long enjoyed; they simply replaced, through the restructuring of the modes of production and appropriation, the layers of illusion used by the nobility (mysticism of symbols, politico-religious illusions like the divine right of kings, etc.) with naked self-interest, direct exploitation, pseudo-scientific justifications for racialization and inhuman brutality and open, unashamed oppression. Human worth was reduced to mere exchange value, and all of social life was commoditized for efficient valuation, barter and disposal.

These values made up the basis of "morality" for the U.S. ruling class, and they imposed their values on the whole of society through their enforcement apparatus, "the state." The institutions of U.S. society were structured to orient the population in these notions of "morality" and "law" as well as their underlying basis: *profit and violence*.

In doing so, the U.S. ruling class embedded the illusion into the whole of society that the ruling class's interests and the people's interests were one and the same, thus developing a slavery of the willing. Hierarchical and authoritarian in nature, the function of these institutions was to reproduce these warped values in society as a whole – based on one's class, cultural group and resultant social function – as the supreme rules of social life.

This process of assimilation to the ruling class took its own unique form for each culture and class subject to its domination. For

New Afrikans, it took the form of Jim Crow apartheid lynch law, COINTELPRO, the deliberate application of poverty, the intentional introduction of narcotics, criminalization, "legal" re-enslavement (in mass incarceration) and "civil death."

Throughout each of these eras, we saw racist violence and murder being visited upon us at the hands of the state and aspects of its majority Euro-Amerikan population. Though New Afrikan resistance to the assimilation process has been consistent over the course of our 400-year domestic colonization – including organized self-defense at different periods throughout that history – we have yet to develop and implement a consistent and comprehensive secure community's strategy across the New Afrikan collective in Amerika. Our failure to do so has both maintained our vulnerability to racist violence in the U.S. and emboldened those who perpetuate such attacks upon us to continue to do so.

> (W)hile the economic conditions of an ideology give us an insight into its material base, they offer us no immediate knowledge of its irrational core. Subject to the specific economic conditions of a society, man reproduces the historical economic process in his ideology. By forming ideologies, man re-shapes himself; man's core is to be sought in the process by which he forms ideologies. Thus it is clear that the irrational formation of an ideology also makes man's structure irrational.[5]
>
> – Wilhelm Reich

We watched along with the world the images of Dylann Roof calmly walking into historic Emanuel A.M.E. Church. He sat in fellowship with nine of our sistas and brothas for an hour, then pulled out a gun and slaughtered them like sheep. Moments later he calmly exited the church, completely unmolested, got in his car, and drove away, leaving Rev. C. Pickney, Cynthia Hurd, Rev. D. Simmons Sr., Uzia Jackson, Tywana Sanders, Myra Thompson, Rev. Sharonda G. Singleton, Rev. Depayne M. Doctor and Ethel Lance dead.

This immediately conjured images of another New Arikan church in another time ... of four little New Afrikan girls in an Alabama church murdered by a klansman's bomb. Our minds moved to Trayvon Martin, Emmett Till, Renisha McBride, Eric Garner, John Crawford, Ezell Ford, Omar Abrego, Michael Brown, Tamir Rice, Oscar Grant and so many more, stretching in an unbroken line of corpses all the way back to the Middle Passage. The corresponding actions and organization of the broad masses of New Afrikans seems to reflect a collective irrationality, which could not analyze the core contradictions accurately, and as a result are incapable of developing viable solutions to these contradictions.

Before we can speak of an anti-racist agenda in the U.S., it must be understood that racism and its underlying basis, reactionary racial violence, are ideologies, and these *ideologies* are structural components of U.S. society. They cannot be "reformed" away. They are woven into the superstructure and base of capitalist Amerikka and are foundational components of its culture.

Racism itself, an ideological component of the system of global white supremacy, owes its very existence to New World slavery and the genocide of Native Americans during the U.S. ruling class's primitive accumulation of capital. Racism is a uniquely Amerikan creation, and it is wholly irrational for us to seek to "reform away" the cultural fiber and ideological foundations of a society.

It is even more irrational to seek to affect such change through identifying with its state and looking to its institutions – judicial, legislative, academic, socio-economic etc. – for such reform, when it's the function of the state and these institutions to preserve the Amerikan cultural fiber and defend its ideological foundation – which includes the race-caste system and its underlying basis: racist violence.

It's as though a large swath of the New Afrikan population has been so thoroughly assimilated to the ruling class that they have lost their capacity for rational thought. It is as though they're incapable of thinking outside the dominant power system.

Consider the response of a significant number of our people in the immediate aftermath of Dylan Roof's attack: They clamored for the Confederate battle flag to be removed from the South Carolina State Capitol, instead of clamoring to secure our communities and their institutions from further attacks.

We watched the entire proceedings, as South Carolina Gov. Nikki Haley, a longtime and staunch defender of maintaining the Confederate flag "as a symbol of (their) heritage," shook the hands of the families of those slain as the flag lowering ceremony commenced. We looked upon this sea of humanity outside the South Carolina Capitol begin to cheer as an "honor guard" marched out to respectfully remove this symbol of death, torture, exploitation and hatred of New Afrikans and were amazed at the depth of irrationality in the U.S. mass psychology.

The state's obsession with pomp and pageantry was clearly designed to deepen the delusion that the removal of this flag had any significance whatsoever in the structural racial hatred and institutional white supremacy imbedded – consciously or unconsciously – in the hearts and minds of millions upon millions of Euro-Amerikans.

We noted, as the flag was removed, New Afrikans were shouting, "USA! USA! USA!" and waving tiny U.S. flags, while only a few yards away, over half the crowd – all Euro-Amerikans, all clearly less than joyful – were hoisting Confederate battle flags in every size, while at the front of their crowd, one fellow was hoisting a large U.S. flag in one hand and the Confederate battle flag in the other. As if mirroring our thoughts, the camera panned back to the mixed half of the crowd still blithely shouting "USA! USA!" as if the contradiction only feet away wasn't underscoring the irrationality of both their chant and their celebration.

Between 2005 and 2012, according to a study by USA Today, New Afrikans were murdered by Euro-Amerikan police officers at a rate of twice a week.[6] Every one of those officers had a central commonality: Each of them had a U.S. flag sewn to their uniform. It was almost as though we were looking upon a physical manifestation of the U.S. fascist mass psychology.

We often view the ideology of racism as something separate from us, while failing to analyze how our core psychology has been affected by it. At the same time they were removing the Confederate flag from the South Carolina Capitol, it was being erected in millions of homes across the U.S. Amazon.com reported a 3,260 percent increase in sales of "Old Dixie" the day it was removed.

It would have been more rational to leave that flag right where it was, as a constant reminder of just what type of sick society we live in and our need to organize ourselves for self-defense and social transformation. The Confederate battle flag is just that – a symbol of Amerikan's willingness to fight to preserve institutional racism as a structural component of U.S. capitalist society ... just like the U.S. flag.

Consider this: In response to the massacre at Emanuel A.M.E., "Black Lives Matter" was spray-painted on the statue of a Confederate general. The response of Klansmen to this was to burn down six New Afrikan churches in five states. U.S. mass media mentioned a NAIM formation was holding a rally in South Carolina; the Ku Klux Klan's response was to hold a march and rally through downtown Charleston, complete with national media coverage and police escorts to ensure their security.

The same way the U.S. government views ISIS or Al Qaeda as terrorist groups bent on the destruction of their nation and interests, the New Afrikan people in Amerikka view the KKK. There is nothing ISIS has done that the KKK hasn't done to New Afrikans in Amerika – only the Klan carried these atrocities out with much more frequency over a much longer period of time.

However, if ISIS were to march and rally in downtown Charleston, S.C., they would be subject to immediate arrest and imprisonment under the U.S. Freedom Act, National Security Act and other "anti-terrorism" laws. But if the KKK does the same, they're provided the full protection of the U.S. Constitution – armed police escorts and national media exposure.

Amazingly – or perhaps NOT so amazingly – the local NAACP president asserted, "They have a First Amendment right to do so," and he supports their right to exercise it. What is the difference between ISIS and the KKK? One is all Euro-Amerikan, Christian, kills New Afrikans and is protected by the U.S. state; the other is primarily Arabic Muslim, targets Amerikans and Europeans, and is summarily killed by the U.S. state.

In the face of such gross contradictions, do you truly believe "Black Lives Matter" to the U.S. state? Racism and racist violence will continue to re-invent itself as long as the ruling class and state in power remain in power.

Part 2
Racism will continue to exist so long as the belief in the concept of 'race' and the material reality underlying it exists. It's this belief which allows racism to appear as totally autonomous (independent) of the economic relations it serves: capitalism. Unless and until it is uprooted, its forms will change, and its practices will ebb and flow, following the needs of its base, the political requirements of the oppressive state, and the forms and levels of struggle engaged by the people.

Must racism be challenged? Yes. Does 'race' have a certain kind of 'reality'? Yes, but, what we fail to focus on is that 'race' is only as 'real' as our consciousness and our practices will allow it to be.[7]

—Atiba (James Yaki Sayles)

Understanding the primary purpose of "racism" (to prevent broad class cooperation across cultural lines and to destroy unity amongst oppressed cultural groups with common interests) ensures that we develop strategies which protect our communities from the effects of this psychosis, without compromising our class unity or prospects of social cooperation. "Understanding that racism is a manufactured concept aids us in fighting it from the proper perspective – rationally and scientifically."

"Combatting racism" is the conscious engagement of a fiction which has been granted material force in the world through its ideological structure. We are struggling against an illusion which only exists in the minds of man and woman. But much like superstition and the supernatural, it imposes itself on reality solely through our belief. Though irrational and unscientific, racism is nevertheless like the ghosts and ghouls that haunt our dreams, very lethal – and as such, it must be defended against ... rationally.

Rationality is a hallmark of resistance to fascist assimilation. It is an indication of the peoples' capacity to see its relationship to the productive system and social life as it actually is – and respond to it accordingly. It is not the existence of racist murder, violent atrocities, state sponsored terror and national indifference to the plight of New Afrikans in Amerika which should shock the conscience – that is all fairly standard in the U.S. It is the suicidal irrationality of our collective response to it which should concern us all.

A cursory analysis of the New Afrikan experience in Amerika from 1619 to the present clearly reveals Amerikans socially control, exploit, contain and kill New Afrikans as a matter of national policy. It is a policy that has evolved to maintain its function through every change in mode of production – from manual labor to industrialization, mechanization and computerization to financialization – pursued invariably through each, ever emerging, ever resilient.

Yet, in the face of tragedy after tragedy, be it racist police murdering us or psychopathic wannabe "Rhodesians" massacring us, we have yet to collectively commit to self-defense and securing our communities.

A primary question asked on tests measuring human intelligence is "If a faucet is running and a sink is overflowing, what do you do first?" (a) Get a mop and clean up the water, or (b) Turn off the faucet"? Of course you secure the faucet first. Otherwise you will be mopping indefinitely.

Similarly, what should we as a people do first? Organize ourselves so that our communities are no longer vulnerable to racist violence, or, continue to plead and organize within the same system that is responsible for the preservation and perpetuation of that racist violence?

The answer would seem obvious – yet it is not reflected in our social practice. Great effort has gone into organizing efforts like The Black Youth Project (BYP100), Dream Defenders, and reorganizing the NAACP, mobilizing hundreds of thousands of our people to hold elected officials accountable, organize rallies and direct action campaigns to raise the peoples' consciousness, garner media attention, holding voter registration drives, organizing on social networks, and developing legislation in hopes of ending collective oppression. All very good and very important work ... the same work that we have been doing since "Reconstruction" ... mopping the floor.

It's important that no one misunderstand our point here: The floor does need to be mopped ... just not while the faucet's still running. Yes, prayer and faith are vital aspects of our culture and solidarity in such times of tribulation – but they are a poor defense against bullets. And a reliance on the benevolence of those citizens who are either responsible for our national oppression or who benefit and have historically benefited from it is simply irrational.

We overestimate the power of conversation and the benevolence of the state and those who benefit from our oppression, because, on this very basic level, we will not call this what it really is: hate!

We must defend ourselves against their hate. We must secure our communities – now! Any other course is irrational adventurism ... just more floor mopping.

Even more irrational is the response of many of the warriors among us. As if to rub salt in the wounds of our own contradictions, the story the news ran immediately following that of the massacre at

Emanuel A.M.E. was of the epidemic of New Afrikan on New Afrikan gang violence plaguing Chicago.

As we watch these images of our brothas, sistas and children murdering one another across Chitown, we realized that it could have been Watts, Cleveland, Oakland, Baltimore or Southeast San Diego that they were talking about. In the face of unprecedented racist attacks on our communities from agents of the state, self-styled vigilantes or run of the mill racist psychopaths, our response is to help them out by murdering one another over hood, set, turf or (drug) sack.

We can't be serious!? Actively participating in our own genocide, in the face of non-stop assault on our humanity, is a classic example of the hate that hate has produced. Our inability to be able to look at each other and see a reflection of ourselves – the absence of a cultural kinship – is a consequence of our being under the influence of white supremacy.

Division and disunity is weakness and vulnerability, but unlike a weak buffalo on a savannah that has become weak through illness, age or injury, ours is a willful weakness, a deliberate vulnerability and, as such, it is reversible. The solution is to create a qualitative transformation in one social extreme – in this case, disunity-born weakness – by quantitatively increasing its opposite: UNITY.

It should never be easy to harm us – any of us. We must put our collective survival before our petty self-interests.

Part 3

The essence of this deterrence strategy is the following: when someone attacks you or threatens you, you make it clear that they will suffer in return. He – or she – may be stronger, he may be able to win battles, but you will make him pay for each victory.... You make him understand that every time he bothers you, he can expect damage, even if it is small. The only way to make you stop ... is for him to stop attacking you. You are like a wasp on his skin: Most people leave wasps alone.[8]

—Robert Greene

In the aftermath of the Charleston Massacre, some Blacks in open carry states began carrying arms. According to Pew Research, the number of Blacks viewing gun ownership as a good thing rose in two years from 29 to 54 percent nationwide in 2015.[9] This was a rational response to a clear and present danger to our communities.

We must protect ourselves and our communities from these attacks by securing our communities. And that includes developing self-defense groups within our communities, safe zones that encompass public spaces for our children and grandchildren to play in, where our mothers and grandmothers, fathers and grandfathers, wives and lovers, friends and neighbors can engage in other areas of social life without fear of violent death by the hands of those of whose responsibility it is to protect them and our communities. We must also work diligently to overcome the mentality that has us held captive.

One of the chief psychological factors which have long undermined a collective policy of self-defense within the New Afrikan community, communities of color and poor communities is the state's insistence that violence is their sole province. Non-violence and passive acceptance of brutality is popularized in the media, revered in discourse and monuments by the state.

This is not by happenstance.

It is the historic continuation of the deliberate imposition of psychological weakness and submission to white supremacy begun in the "man-breaking, slave-making" process centuries ago. To reverse this process requires we practice its opposite: *self-defense and armed struggle.*

The act of securing our communities and reclaiming our humanity has a dialectically progressive effect on our people and on us all as well.

We begin to shed the capitalist delusions and colonial psychosis which have been imposed on us through the assimilation process. We begin to see the true nature of hate. We see past the shadow, which it is, on to the unequal social and economic relationships of the capitalist system which is actually casting it.

We begin to see our manufactured animosities and sub-culture divisions as aspects of our national oppression and, through this realization, glimpse the prospect of a new form of social life. This is what *functional unity* looks like.

Functional unity is both a psychological state and social act; it is the conscious determination that one's subjective animosities or active hostilities within our collective are subordinate to the survival of our people and humanity. It is consciously acting on a daily basis to ensure the welfare and survival of each other.

If our national oppression has taught us anything, it's that the only "rights" we have are those that we can enforce. Our rights can only be enforced through self-defense.

Attacks upon poor communities, both physical and socio-political, are not abating but increasing. In the months of October, November and December 2015, just around the St. Louis area, seven New Afrikan churches were burned to the ground and, in the previous August, Yogi was assassinated. There is no area of social life in Amerika where New Afrikan mortality is not under threat, no place in this land where New Afrikan life is not undervalued, no other rational conclusion we can reach than we must educate, organize and mobilize our communities and ourselves for self-defense and our own security.

Think on these things. They are cause for great meditation.

CHAPTER

ELEVEN

JOKA HESHIMA JINSAI

Trayvon, Christian, Jason, Gerardo, Kendrec and
Nine Children in Afghanistan

132

JOKA HESHIMA JINSAI

Trayvon, Christian, Jason, Gerardo, Kendrec and Nine
Children In Afghanistan:

"Racism" is used to justify and facilitate the exploitation of
peoples, and it's based on the false belief that humanity is
divided into a plurality of 'races' that stand in relation to
each other as 'inferior' or 'superior' based on physical
and/or cultural differences. There are no 'races' – only
people(s), groups of people(s), united and distinguished by
common history (social development), habits, interests etc.
– sometimes we call all of this … ideology.[1]
                                        – James Yaki Sayles

Greetings, brothers and sisters. A firm, warm, and solid embrace is
extended to you all. In the past year we have witnessed a
succession of murderous assaults against the people from various
segments of the bourgeois apparatus reflecting a common character
structure: The authoritarian psychology. In July 2011 a group of
racists beat Jason Smith, a young New Afrikan man, to death in
Louisiana; in February 2012 Trayvon Martin was murdered by a racist
vigilante in Sanford, Fla.; that same month Christian Gomez was
allowed to die of starvation-related complications by guards while on

hunger strike at Corcoran State Prison in California; in March 2012, 17 people, nine of them children, were slaughtered by a U.S. Army Staff Sgt. Bales in two Afghan villages as they lay down to sleep; that same month Kendrec McDade was slain by racist police in Pasadena, Calif.; in April 2012 Gerardo Perez-Ruiz was murdered by border vigilantes in Eloy, Ariz.

Each of these atrocities can be traced back to a single warped thought process. The U.S. Fascist Mass psychology is the key inhibiting factor of social progress in this nation and the origin of sadistic violence in the modern world. Though all of these atrocities offend the humanity of each of us, we'll highlight two of the cases to illustrate the etiological correlation of racist, xenophobic, sadistic violence and authorization psychology.

Imagine if you will, you are walking home one evening from the local convenience store with a can of tea and a bag of skittles for your younger brother. You're looking forward to the Miami Heat game with your father when some strange man drives up and accosts you: "Hey! What are you doing around here? Come here! You need to explain your presence to my satisfaction."

You're a young man, a child really, and you don't know who this guy is. He could be a kidnapper, pedophile, racist murderer – you don't know. "I'm going home, man." And you attempt to continue on your way … but he prevents you.

You're frightened and confused as your fight or flight response kicks in; an altercation ensues and you scream for help as this strange white man pulls a gun. He aims at your chest and your screams of terror are cut off by the thunderclap of a gunshot, and the shock of pain as the hot bullet rips into your flesh slamming you backwards. You fall to the ground feeling the wet pavement under your cheek. As your life flows out of your body, your young eyes glaze to darkness as you die...

You open them to see your six brothers and sisters in the common room of your father's home as your mother and aunt prepare everyone for sleep in your small village in Afghanistan. Your sister makes a joke, and as your siblings giggle, the night is sundered by the sound of rifle fire... and it's coming from *inside* your home.

You hear your Uncle scream as no human should and then, out of the darkness like some evil djinn from a fairy tale, steps the U. S. soldier aiming his rifle at your Moma. He fires and pieces of her and your aunt spray the wall. The sound is so loud the screams of your siblings are drowned out as you all attempt, futilely, to flee to the other corner and he orders you all face down on the ground. A boot slams down on your back pinning your tiny body to the earth. You hear a slitting sound then a wet slamming sound, and the gurgles and groans of your siblings as they are butchered like cattle. Your fear is drowned by confusion as you flail mentally to grasp why the Amerikan is killing you all. His foot slams down on your tiny shoulder again, crushing the bone as you scream and turn your head up and around as the sight of the large bloody combat knife fills up your entire world. In a flash of pain and horror, the world is no more...

You wake to the familiar ache of hunger in your small cell in Corcoran State Prison ASU. You've been on hunger strike, and now something is wrong. Your heartbeat is racing, you can't get enough breath. You knock on the wall to alert your neighbor to your distress. Soon the rest of the guys on hunger strike begin to kick and bang on the doors.

The prison guards can clearly hear the yells of "Man down" and your cell number as a sharp pain grips your chest and abdomen and you fall to the cold cell floor. The calls of "Man down!" and kicking on cell doors becomes more insistent as if the others can sense the grip of death closing around your body. The guards continue to ignore these calls.

Fear and panic seize you as your body no longer obeys your commands. You've not eaten in many days. It was the only way to bring attention to the reality of the U.S. domestic torture program being carried out in ASU (Administrative Segregation Unit) and SHU (Security Housing Unit) torture units in California. That coupled with your illness has weakened your body too much to resist the draw of the veil.

It seems like so much time has passed since those around you began calling for aid to help you and none has come. None will ever come as you realize you are about to die ... It hurts so much, perhaps death is not such a bad thing ... Your eyes begin to flutter ... They open and shut once more ... but they see only emptiness ... You have passed on ...

These nightmare imaginings, which were the reality for Trayvon Martin, Christian Gomez, nine children in Afghanistan, and all those victims we named at the outset, all have a common psycho-social correlation in their aggressors: All these instances involved social expressions of the same warped character structure; all these instances involved the murder of people of color by Euro-Americans or repressive forces of the U.S. state consistent with that historic dynamic; all these instances involved, despite mass outcry, at least the attempt at tacit justification or explanation by authoritarian interests in the U.S.

I have included in my previous discussions the pathology that has been created by our failure to deal with the legacy of racism and the capitalist authoritarian psychology that spawned it. It has claimed five more victims here and 17 more in a single night in Afghanistan. Trayvon Martin and Christian Gomez did not have to die. But they did. George Zimmerman and CSP-Corcoran ASU guards both share the identical psychological character structure of authoritarian man, reinforced by their particular stations in the U.S. social arrangement: the dominance of white male privilege and state power.

George Zimmerman, an affluent member of an exclusive gated community, clearly exemplifying the perceived supremacy of his Euro-American parentage and economic station, felt completely justified in pursuing this New Afrikan child that he identified as "Black" to the 911 operator. He then stated, "They always get away," just before hunting down, accosting and subsequently murdering this poor child.

Much of America does not get that within the New Afrikan community there is still a discussion held between parents and male Afrikan children about the dangers they face in the larger society because of their sable skin. For any that believe this is an exaggeration, the execution of Trayvon, Jason and Kendrec is proof these fears continue to be well grounded in truth and prudence. The fact that Mr. Zimmerman continues to feel justified in executing Trayvon, as evidenced by his self-serving statements to Trayvon's parents at the bail hearing, should chill all of you reading this. The state released him.

The irrational core of such justifications lies in the racial dehumanization of New Afrikans (males in particular) in the U.S. This dehumanizing dynamic is embodied in the historical development of property relations in the U.S.: a wealth surplus cultivated on the backs of Afrikan slaves working stolen Native American lands.

The unique ideological basis of capitalist economic development in the U.S., which incorporates the race-caste system as a vital component of the class structure, created a corresponding character structure that this process reproduces and re-enforces in its citizens. There has never been a conflict between democracy and racial oppression, inequality and exploitation in the mind of authoritarian man in Amerika. The pathological dehumanization of racism is the central component which allowed Zimmerman to not only murder a New Afrikan child for walking in "his" neighborhood, but to justify doing so as "self-defense" and have that "justification" echoed by the Sanford Police Department. Such irrational reasoning has an origin.

In "The Ignoble Paradox of Modernity," of Cornel West's, *The Modern Reader* , West states, "Racialized persons and racist practices were systemized and canonized principally owing to the financial interests and psychic needs that sustained the slave trade and New World slavery."[2] It is this racial component of economic exploitation and conquest which is the developmental foundation of U.S. society still celebrated on Columbus Day. The irrational mentality of George

Zimmerman did not fall from the sky. It was developed from the authoritarian mass psychology and national ideology of the U.S.

While a historical analysis of U.S. economic conditions gives us a glimpse into the material basis for racist ideology, it provides little insight into its irrational core – how it got there in this warped form today. Subject to the socio-economic conditions of U.S. capitalist society, Amerikan man reproduces those unique historical economic processes in his ideology.

This is why some three centuries after the "Willie Lynch method" was introduced to increase the productive output and relative safety of enslaving Afrikans in the Amerikkka's, the same twisted psychic structures that process created continue to be reproduced in both New Afrikans (the slave mentality, inferiority complexes, self-hatred) and Euro-Amerikans (authoritarian white male privilege, superiority complexes, hatred of other human phenotypes) in the U.S. today.

Ideologies reshape man's being; we discover his material core by analyzing the process by which he forms ideologies. The toxic historical process and development of U.S. patriarchal authoritarianism exemplified by its brutal enslavement of Afrikans, bloody extermination of Native Americans, conquest and annexation of lands and resources, from Northern Mexico to the Philippine Islands, continue to give rise to the psychic certainty of additional atrocities in those who maintain the ideological "traditions" of the "Amerikan way" today.

You see, the irrational formation of an ideology also makes man's character structure irrational. Thus the genesis of the pathologically warped reasoning of Zimmerman; that he, not this frightened child, was "justified" in "defending himself." Such a position is an indictment of the modern U.S. authoritarian mass psychology itself.

To be sure, for weeks we've watched corporate mass media put forward theories of justification which absolve this gun toting, self-appointed "neighborhood-watch commander" of culpability in murdering this child – even going so far as attempting to disparage Trayvon's character with such descriptions as "He was a troubled youth with behavior problems" in one breath, while dialoging on the analysis and re-analysis of the police video of Zimmerman's head injury in the next.

The underlying message of the corporate mass media was given unvarnished clarity only days later in a tweet by a white New Jersey police officer, who said of Trayvon, "Act like a thug; die like a thug." This simple articulation of the modern dehumanization of New Afrikans in Amerika by the authoritarian apparatus was the guiding ethos of George Zimmerman and the Sanford police.

To those with this twisted mindset, Trayvon was not a "human" child walking home from the store to watch the game with his family; he was "one of them," "Black," "they," a "thug" – something other than, and inferior to, Zimmerman himself. In his mind he was justified in pursuing Trayvon, justified in accosting him, justified in murdering him because George Zimmerman was an upper-middle class white man "protecting" his community, and Trayvon just some "Black thug" in a hoodie.

This is really the type of sick, twisted rationalization that was proffered by Zimmerman and initially accepted by the Sanford police. Even when it was clear the nexus of protestation had forced the reactionary state to cleave with the authoritarian social imperative and finally arrest Zimmerman, instead of focusing on the self-evident atrocity of Trayvon's murder and inexcusable delay in the state seeking redress, the authoritarian regime used this moment for law enforcement to sing its own accolades and re-enforce the authoritarian status quo by stressing the position that the national outcry at this one man lynching was not a factor in the state's decision to prosecute.

They verified it by allowing Zimmerman to deposit $15k with a bail bondsman and just walk out of jail scot free, as though such a warped human hiding behind the "stand your ground" statute does not pose a threat to the safety and lives of others. Just as disturbing, only weeks later, it was discovered Zimmerman was not having such a great economic difficulty as he'd led the court to believe. He had raised some $250k online for his "defense." The fact that so many Amerikans donated money to Zimmerman in just a few short weeks that he was able to amass a quarter million dollars is definitive proof of the mass psychosis of the authoritarian psychology in Amerika.

The "stand your ground" policy that is the law in Florida does include the Trayvon Martins of this nation; how can it not? With this in mind, how can any rational person entertain, even for a second, the explanation of Zimmerman, who's admitted to pursuing and confronting this child before slaying him?

We live in a society that has never committed itself to changing the way that it thinks. The same social, political and economic forces that created the mentality that lynched Emmett Till and later James Byrd is the same system that is responsible for what is called racial profiling today. This is the same type of thinking that resulted in the murders of Kendrec McDade and Gerardo Perez-Ruiz earlier this year.

These are the same forces that created the hate which bombed a church in Birmingham, Alabama, that claimed the lives of four little New Afrikan girls attending Sunday school in 1963; the same hate which killed James Chaney, Andrew Goodman and Michael Schwerner in Philadelphia, Mississippi, in 1964; the same hate that murdered Jason Smith in Louisiana in July of 2011.

Trayvon Martin's black skin is what put him on the radar of Zimmerman and he said as much to the 911 operator. The dispatcher specifically told him not to pursue Trayvon, but Zimmerman hunted Trayvon anyway because he felt he had the authority to do so. That authoritarian mindset had fatal results. It was definitely upheld as a U.S. cultural more when Zimmerman was ultimately acquitted.

The outrage that has been and continues to be expressed is justified. But it is not enough to demand justice. George Zimmerman is a symptom of a diseased society. We have legalized hate with the legislation of racial profiling and laws such as "stand your ground,"

Arizona's anti-immigrant statues and "gang" injunctions on entire communities of color. It is a crisis of culture, a manifestation of the malignant sickness of bourgeois society. The maintenance of this pathology is not reserved for domestic atrocities – no; the U. S. is an Empire. The effects of its unique brand of patriarchal authoritarian psychosis are *global* in nature. It's reared its head in massacre after massacre in U.S. conflicts from the slaughter at Wounded Knee, to the napalm Killing fields of Vietnam and Cambodia...to a night on March 11, 2012, in two tiny villages in Afghanistan where seventeen Afghan civilians, nine of them children, were shot, stabbed and burned to death by U.S. Army Staff Sgt. Robert Bales. Similar to the case of Trayvon and Zimmerman, news reports focused less on the families of these nine babies who were slaughtered by this "man-chine", and more on some rationalization as to what may have "provoked" Bales. "Perhaps it was post-traumatic stress, a traumatic brain injury, repeated warzone deployments after being passed over for promotion in the midst of financial hardship" – all of these have been put forward over a backdrop of family, neighbors and supporters who "simply don't believe he could be involved in such a terrible and heartbreaking tragedy."

What must be understood about the authoritarian mass psychology in the U.S. is it is an ideology of domination and self-suppression whose underlying basis is violence.

U.S. military occupations, be they imperialistic or colonial, have always maintained domination by the infliction of terror, despair, and disproportionate deaths on the native population; simultaneously drawing stark psychological lines in the minds of its soldiers between themselves and the Indigenous population which *always* leads to dehumanizing characterizations. If the Native differs from the dominant segment of the U.S. race-caste (i.e. white male) the dehumanization of the Native is then reflexive. This is an outgrowth of a key aspect of authoritarian mass psychology I have *not* discussed in previous pieces; *the mechanization of authoritarian man/woman.* Like authoritarian psychology itself, this process took thousands of years and finds its origins in man's efforts to disassociate himself from the animal as he developed technology and religion. Man's capacity for abstract reasoning and moral or mystical justification for immoral or sadistic behavior is the root of this authoritarian view of life, and the primary basis by which he is differentiated from the animal Wilhelm Reich observed in chapter twelve of *The Mass Psychology of Fascism*:

> Man's life is dichotomized: One part of his life is determined by biological laws (sexual gratification, consumption of foods relatedness to nature); the other part of his life is determined by *the machine* civilization (mechanical ideas about his own (self) organization, his superior position in the animal Kingdom. This racial or class attitude toward other human groups, valuations about ownerships science, religion, etc.). His being an animal and his not being an animal: biological roots on the one hand, and technical development on the other hand, cleave man's life and thought.[3]

Western man has thus become a robot – a "man-chine" – carrying out the dictates of authoritarian interests with mechanistic efficiency and detachment.

There exists no more mechanistic organization than the military in the U.S. Throughout U.S. history, the Amerikan military has professed to be doing everything from "advancing civilization", to "defending freedom" while committing genocide on the Great Plains, or dropping napalm on children in the Inchon Valley (Vietnam). Yet this contradiction between the soldiers "noble" values and his actual behavior has never inspired any great controversy in and of itself, it is only when the masses begin to organize and move against the ideological foundations of these acts (as they did in the 60s and 70s) that *any* attention is given to this irrationality in reactionary man. On the contrary, as we saw with Sgt. Bales, the reaction of the U. S. masses is to seek *justifications* or "reasonable" explanations to mitigate or explain away the uncomfortable truth: that an irrational mass-murderer lies just beneath the thin veneer of "patriotism and honor" in the mind of *every* authoritarian man.

Just as the George Zimmerman's of this society are the reproduction of elitist white male privilege in the upper middle class, so are soldiers, like Sgt. Bales, the psychological reproduction of the same interest in dominance of the occupied population. As I've explained in other works, the reproduction of authoritarian mass psychology in oppressed segments of society itself is the basis of the oppressed submission to exploitation and inhibition to resistance or Revolution.

In an occupied nation, the authoritarian psychological structure expresses itself differently. It speaks the language of brute force and bloody violence. The soldier, by his physical presence and intervention into the daily lives of the occupied keeps the Native in check with the bullet, the blade, and the boat. There is no desire to mask the authoritarian reality – "The Matrix" is not employed – the domination is upheld by bringing the reality of deadly force into the homes and hearts of the occupied. Prolonged activation in the "man-chine" node of war strips away the illusion of "moralistic values" from the mind of the reactionary soldier leasing only its underlying basis: sadistic violence.

This is merely a continuation of the historic manifestations of white supremacy seen in U. S. Cavalrymen cutting the breasts off Native American women to make tobacco pouches or U.S. special forces operators setting fire to Vietnamese children in front of their families to coerce them into providing information on Viet-Cong guerrillas; to U.S. service men/women in Iraq and Afghanistan posing with, or urinating on, the dead bodies of "insurgent's"…to Sgt. Bales going on a nighttime stroll to massacre seventeen innocent men, women and children. According to Sgt. Bales, he had no memory of the massacre itself. I contend that's because he was functioning from his unconscious mechanistic, authoritarian core. If we contrast the reaction of corporate mass-media and many here in the U.S., to the atrocities committed by Sgt. Bales and that given to the massacre of twenty-two Norwegian youth by white nationalists, and mass-murderer Anders Breivik, we cannot escape the double standard, though both atrocities stem from the *same* authoritarian mass psychology.

The core authoritarian psychology that gives social validity to these warped mindsets must itself be eradicated. We will continue experiencing these atrocities until such time as the minds of the masses are transformed, until we realize a victorious revolutionary change in this society.

But this pathology finds its most indifferent expression not in the gated communities of the upper middle class, or the fog of war. No, it finds its most indifferent expression in prisons. Over the past 30 years, with tacit state sanction and support, the victims' rights lobby and prison industrial complex have waged a successful dehumanization campaign on those who've abrogated "the law." The compulsion of socio-economic desperation, race-class disenfranchisement, and intentional underdevelopment of specific segments of the underclass – overwhelmingly New Afrikan, Latino and Native American – have been irrationally discounted as the origin of "crime," and the onus for survival activities has been placed solely on the shoulders of the individual offender.

From this artificial social perspective has arisen the myth of the sub-human, predatory, criminal offender.

Those consigned to U.S. prisons do not simply lose their physical freedom; they lose their social designation as fellow "humans." Society views prisoners the same way we view vermin – as something other than human, repugnant and unworthy of compassion. Christian Gomez discovered this with fatal results. Prison, as a tool of social control and race-caste containment, has always been a key component of U.S. capitalism, but the broad based, systematic dehumanization of prisoners has expanded in direct proportion to the economic expansion of the prison industrial slave complex.

In the 2010 annual report of Corrections Corporation of America the world's largest private prison purveyor, they state:

> The demand for our facilities and services could be adversely affected by the relaxation of enforcement efforts, leniency in conviction or parole standards and sentencing practices.... For instance, any changes with respect to drugs or controlled substances or illegal immigration could affect the number of people arrested, convicted and sentenced, thereby potentially reducing the demand for correctional facilities to house them.[4]

The CCPOA (California Correctional Peace Officers Association), GEO Group [the world's second largest private prison purveyor], and the Fraternal Order of Police have parroted these same lines openly in their lobbying efforts at the state and federal level. Do you not see the inherent contradiction in a public safety apparatus whose speculative profits and salaries are attached to maximizing criminal offenders, not reducing them?

This view they hold of prisoners and potential prisoners as commodities by the various aspects of the prison industry – both public and private – provides a compelling economic motivation for maintaining that social dehumanization in the overall populace. Seventy percent of all TV programing is crime and punishment content, from "Cops" to "Judge Judy," from "Law and Order: SVU" to "Blue Bloods" and countless others – all re-enforcing the message of corporate mass media and the labor aristocracy of prison guard unions like the CCPOA that prisoners are not humans but some subspecies of bipedal animal entirely separate from humanity itself. This is particularly pronounced in American paramilitary organizations like police or prison guards and is a manifestation of the mechanization of authoritarian man in the West.

There is thus no contradiction in the mind of the prison guard in upholding their oath to the Constitution's noble humanistic ideals and dehumanizing imprisoned citizens. The warped character structure of the authoritarian psychology to differentiate itself from the "animal" –

"the criminal" – makes that dehumanization a simple economic determination for prison staff, an almost reflexive psychological process intimately connected to their economic empowerment, socio-political prestige and influence.

That New Afrikans and Latinos make up 75 percent of the prison population, but a scant 26 percent of the national population gives a corresponding race-caste "justification" to this dehumanizing dynamic in their minds. So ignoring Christian Gomez' – and the entire unit's – pleas for help as he died in agony was no great feat for the prison guards.

That the only outcry that has been heard has come from the relatively small community of social progressives reveals the immutable truth of the pervasiveness of the authoritarian mass psychology in the U.S.

Society's support for this evil in service to power and privilege is exposed by their apathy and silence. Despite his mistakes in life, Christian Gomez was not only human, he was a hero, and those of us who are principled people cannot allow his sacrifice to be forgotten. Much has been said about the medical problems that he had which contributed to his tragic death. However, the question that we must ask is: How dreadful must the conditions under which he and others were housed have been that Christian would commit himself to starving himself given his medical condition?

How sick and twisted must the core psychology of our nation be that so few of us have expressed our horror and outrage at the prison guards who just stood idly by, ignoring screams for help, and let him die in agony? How long will we allow racism and the authoritarian psychology at the core of those guards' character structures govern our cultural mores? The same sadism in service to the authoritarian imperative laid waste to the peaceful protest at Attica in 1971; gunned down W.L. Nolen and other freedom fighters in the late '60s and let them bleed out on the yard, feeding the melancholy history of Soledad State Prison; assassinated George L. Jackson in San Quentin on August 21, 1971, ... and allowed Christian Gomez to die horribly in Corcoran ASU on Feb. 2, 2012.

Only in struggle, in actively educating those who are unconscious, organizing those who are conscious and mobilizing the advanced elements against the authoritarian psychosis will we effect meaningful change in the ideology of hate and sadistic violence which is at the core of authoritarian man's character. It is incumbent upon all freedom loving people to change the culture in which we live. Institutional racism, by whatever name it is called, must be confronted and destroyed wherever it rears its ugly head.

As I have stated before, you – the people – are the greatest force on this planet. You have the power to change this society and the world you live in now, to dictate the kind of world we all live in the future. The power to change the culture that has already taken so much from us ... and of us, is in your hands.

The NCTT and NARN (New Afrikan Revolutionary Nationalist Collective Think Tank), both here in Corcoran SHU and Pelican Bay SHU, have put forward practical programs and platforms for all of us to build toward a brighter world. From the Amend the 13th: Abolish Legal Slavery in Amerika Movement and three pilot programs of the Autonomous Infrastructure Mission (A.I.M.) – CCE (Closed Circuit Economic Initiative), Sustainable Community Agricultural Commune; Youth Community Action Program – developed here; to the glorious efforts put forward by NCTT Chairman Sitawa Nantambu Jamaa and Abdul Olugbala Shakur, such as The Prisoners Human Rights Movement and The Assata Alert Network give us all the tools and institutions capable of forging the transfer culture necessary to turn the tide of history. By taking up these tools and supporting these efforts, we consciously act to shatter the chains of the authoritarian psychosis, to free the minds of the masses – to free ourselves.

Let us end this discussion with these words echoed down the corridors of history as a basis for a lasting solution to these ills of society:

The commune. The central citywide revolutionary culture. But who will build the commune that will guide the people into a significant challenge to property rights? Carving out a commune in the central city will involve claiming certain rights as our own – out front. Rights that have not been respected to now. Property rights. It will involve building a political, social and economic infrastructure, capable of filling the vacuum that has been left by the establishment ruling class and pushing the occupy forces of the enemy culture from our midst.... The revolutionary is outlawed ... Revolution is illegal. It's against the law. It's prohibited. It will not be allowed. It is clear that the revolutionary is a lawless man (or woman). The outlaw and the lumpen will make the revolution. The people, the workers, will adopt it. This must be the new order of things, after the fact of the modern industrial fascist state.[5]

– George Jackson

You will find no class or category more aware, more embittered, desperate or dedicated to the ultimate remedy – revolution. The most dedicated, the best of our kind – you'll find them in the Folsom's, San Quentin's and Soledad's.[6]

– George L. Jackson

Trayvon, Christian, Kendrec, Gerardo, Jason and those nine children in Afghanistan will never know justice as long as the authoritarian psychology and ideology of hate responsible for murdering them is allowed to persist. There is only one sure cure. You are no longer ignorant to its reality or origin.

Will you continue to stand idly by, content to submit to the bonds of the ruling 1 percent, submitting to conformity, turning a blind eye to the evil pervading the very fabric of society? Or will you stand with us and those who dare to change the nature and structure of capitalist society, dare to change the culture of hate, dare to struggle, dare to win?

Your choice will determine the course of history. The spirits of Trayvon, Christian, Kendrec, Gerardo, Jason and those nine Afghan babies are watching all of us with an interested eye. What will you show them?

Think on these things. They are cause for great meditation.

Until we win or don't lose.

CHAPTER TWELVE

STEVE MARTINOT

STEVE MARTINOT

The following chapter articles by Steve Martinot highlight the case of Abdul Olugbala Shakur, who spent decades in solitary confinement.

Steve Martinot has been a human rights activist for most of his life. As a union organizer, community organizer, and anti-war organizer, including Latin America solidarity work, he has worked as a machinist and truck driver, and taught literature and cultural studies at the University of Colorado and San Francisco State University. He is the author of *The Machinery of Whiteness, The Rule of Racialization,* and *Forms in the Abyss: A Philosophical Bridge Between Sartre and Derrida.* He lives in Berkeley, California, leads seminars on the structures of racialization in the United States, and is active in a neighborhood assembly and participatory budget movement.

Prisons, Gangs, Witchhunts and White Supremacy

My brotha, I don't intend to give up. I will continue to promote the New Afrikan Independence Movement and the Republic of New Afrika via New Afrikan Revolutionary Nationalism (NARN). I will continue to coordinate the GJU as well as the BAOC. I will not allow these racist guards to criminalize our movement or our political activities, especially Black August!

> – Abdul Olugbala Shakur, in a letter to a friend (GJU is the George Jackson University; BAOC stands for Black August Organizing Committee).

The Process

There is a trick that the California prison administration (hereafter "Admin") pulls on African Americans in prison. It is to charge them with gang activity if they refer to "George Jackson" or any of his writings or ideas or to the "Republic of New Afrika" or the politics of New Afrikans.

Any such reference will be interpreted to mean one is a member of a group called the Black Guerrilla Family (BGF) and thus guilty of promoting gang activity. Thousands of people, mostly Black and

Brown, have been held in solitary confinement (Security Housing Unit, or SHU) for years and even decades, because "gang activity" constitutes a "security threat to the prison," according to the Admin.

Yet even prisoners held in solitary can be brought up on charges of "gang activity," which is hard to imagine.

Four times in the course of a single year, Abdul Olugbala Shakur, a long-timer in Pelican Bay, has been so charged for letters to friends on the outside. Each time, he was convicted of gang activity and his solitary confinement extended. I recently obtained access to the write-ups of those various hearings, called "Rules Violation Reports." In them, one sees a species of witchhunts in modern form.

Each of these reports follows the same procedure. An officer who had read Shakur's personal mail charges him for making reference to New Afrikan ideas and activity. Because Shakur is a so-called "validated" gang member (an administrative procedure from which there is no appeal), his political references are considered links to the BGF.

These reports then list various bureaucratic procedures preliminary to a hearing, stating how the defendant pleads and stating whether he wants a witness or not. Shakur pleads "not guilty" in each case and, in each case, his request for a witness is denied.

Each report ends with an account of the hearing. It consists of a "finding" – of guilty in each case – and a summary of the evidence provided by an investigating officer. That evidence repeats the original report about Shakur's mail and provides a "synopsis" of the letter intercepted.

These "synopses" refer in part to Shakur's statements and in part to what the officer thinks Shakur means. Thus, the real evidence against Shakur is what the officer thinks. The conclusion that Shakur is involved in gang activity is foregone.

It is all quite routine. However, the testimony against Shakur is interesting and bears some analysis.

First, a little background. There is a special committee called the Institutional Gang Investigators (IGI) whose job is to read the prisoners' mail. In 2010, Shakur had filed a suit against the Admin and the IGI – a case heard by Judge Seeborg in San Francisco – for having intercepted his mail in violation of federal law as well as of his civil and constitutional rights.

He "won" this suit insofar as the Admin was directed to no longer block delivery of mail nor prevent Shakur from receiving personal mail from the outside. This has not stopped the Admin from doing so, however, nor from charging Shakur for what he says in these personal letters.

Two glaring absences "appear" in these reports. The first is the source for proclaiming Shakur a gang member. The second is any proof that the BGF exists as an organization. This doesn't mean it doesn't, but its existence has to be more than an administrative proclamation, if the torture of solitary confinement can be the outcome for the defendant.

The Admin cites no documentary evidence for either claim. Though Shakur contradicts the officer's bland assertions, it is in vain. Shakur's references to ideas remain associated with a "security threat," while all aspects of organizational existence, such as rules, purposes, and membership functions exist only in the officer's claims, without foundation. In other words, the Admin pretends that whatever it says is fact. And that introduces the logic of what is happening here.

The Argument

The intercepted letter in the first report, addressed to an unnamed individual, quotes the warden's response to the decision in Shakur's suit, in which the warden describes the BGF. The charge against Shakur is that, by quoting the warden, he is guilty of promoting gang activity. The warden's statement says:

"The BGF was cofounded in 1966 by George Jackson. Originally the BGF was called the Black Family or Black Vanguard and were associated with the 'Black Mafia.' ... The BGF is the most 'politically' oriented of the major prison gangs. It was formed as a Marxist-Maoist-Leninist revolutionary organization with specific goals to eradicate racism, struggle to maintain dignity in prison and overthrow the U.S. government. [It is hard to keep a straight face, reading this.]

"All members must be Black. Though small in number, the BGF has a very strict death oath which requires a life pledge of loyalty to the gang. Prospective members must be nominated by an existing member. BGF commonly use (sic) different versions of a dragon surrounding a prison tower and holding a correctional officer in its clutches.

They will also use a crossed rifle and machete or the letters BGF."

In his defense, Shakur points out the absurdity of holding against him words the warden had used concerning the Black Mafia, Black Vanguard, etc. "We didn't create those terms," he says. If the words are legitimate in the warden's mouth and criminal in his own, it implies that it is his person, his Blackness or New Afrikanness, that is criminalized, regardless of what he says.

His point, in quoting the warden, is to show that he and the other New Afrikans "unjustly held in solitary confinement" are all political prisoners. "These New Afrikan Revolutionary Brothas have been denied parole or release from the SHU based on their political beliefs and activities."

One searches in vain in this quoted letter for any sense of real threat to the security of the prison. The report states that the letter "was found to contain gang-related writing indicating he [Shakur] is currently active in some level of activity for the BGF. Specifically, in the handwritten portion of the letter, [there are] references to 'New Afrikan Babies,' 'New Afrikan Sistas' and 'New Afrikan Sistahood.' The terms 'New Afrikan Revolutionary,' 'New Man,' 'New Woman' and 'NARN' (New Afrikan Revolutionary Nationalism), are all BGF related terms."

In other words, Shakur is charged with linkages that the Admin makes on its own. It transforms this into "gang activity" insofar as this private letter to a friend attempts to "educat[e] people on the beliefs and ideologies of the BGF" – by quoting the warden.

In a subsequent write-up, the officer claims that Shakur admits to promoting NARN and Black August and that he is "aware" that this type of activity "assists and promotes the BGF." Shakur's position is that NARN and Black August are protected activities, because they are political thoughts and ideas, covered by the First Amendment.

In speaking of Shakur's "awareness" as other than what Shakur says, the officer is speaking for Shakur and thus depriving him of his personhood altogether. There is no defense against someone who speaks for you. If there is no defense, then this "legal" procedure is itself illegal.

Of real substance, however, is the warden's reference to BGF's goals of "eradicating racism and maintaining dignity in prison." These are fundamental demands for human rights. Apparently, such demands constitute a "threat" to prison security.

To add the notion of "overthrowing" the U.S. government from inside prison is laughable, of course, designed to link this "radical" position ("eradicating racism") to the Cold War. It actually succeeds in linking earlier anti-Communist crusades to their own withholding of human rights.

Ultimately, this "gang" is identified by tattoos and logos and references to "New Afrikan" identity. In outlawing a group for what it thinks and for its "colors" (logos and tattoos), we recognize the paradigm of gang injunctions on the outside. In other words, having honed this weapon inside the prison, the government exports it for use in civil society.

Throughout these four hearings, the same boilerplate description of BGF is used, as if repetition was all that was needed to give something status as law. We see this same arbitrary attribution of judiciality and legitimacy in the U.S. government's "no-fly" list. That list was compiled without due process, and deployed without possibility of appeal or review. Administrative decision is simply given the weight of law. Again, what had been developed on the inside becomes an assumed legitimate procedure on the outside.

Similar boilerplate treatment is given by the Admin to ideas such as NARN, Black August and the GJU (George Jackson University), of which Shakur is the self-proclaimed co-founder. In his defense, Shakur refers to the court settlement of his suit wherein the judge had affirmed that NARN and Black August were not BGF activities.

But the Admin ignores this. It simply makes sure its procedure is correct. This priority of procedure over substance occurs routinely on the "outside." It led to the death of Troy Davis despite exonerating evidence. And it has been the court's refusal to admit exonerating evidence in Mumia Abu-Jamal's case, stating that "proper" procedure was followed in his original trial.

The letter that speaks of the George Jackson University, an educational effort led by prisoners from the depths of their confinement, is primarily about how to unite Black people in the broader Black community, for which an end to intra-community violence – especially among street gangs – is essential. The testifying officer admits that this is what Shakur is trying to do.

Shakur is proposing the GJU as a means of bringing peace and unity to street gangs. Because the office has already identified the GJU with the BGF, it reduces this unity project to an instance of BGF control over street gangs and thus a "promotion" of gang violence rather than a project to end it. It is this twist of Admin logic that transforms Shakur's use of the word "gang" into a "security threat."

If the police criminalize efforts to stop street gang violence, it means they want that violence between gangs to continue. The police are aiding and abetting that violence, fostering further criminalization of both street gangs and prisoners who speak about stopping it. Thus, communities and prisons are linked in being beset by anti-social administrations in similar ways.

The Admin's real purpose in these write-ups leaks out through these pages. The concept of Black August is described by the Admin as a commemoration by African Americans of "all of their fallen comrades." It is the officer who says this in his testimony.

What is the Admin admitting in recognizing the fact that there are "fallen comrades?" Fallen in what war? The names of some are listed: Jeffrey Gaulden, Alvin Miller, Cleveland Edwards, W. L. Nolan. All had been killed in prison, shot or beaten to death by guards or the Aryan Brotherhood.

Insofar as such a war would have to be one-sided, with only the Admin – and prisoners in alliance with it – having the possibility of aggression against African American prisoners, is not the Admin admitting that Black people need some kind of defensive organization, both inside and outside the prisons?

The report then states that Black August is an idea "created" by the BGF, thus equating BGF with Black people in general. In other words, Black people are a gang, a security threat. There is the secret behind the spate of police killings that go on in the streets of every U.S. city. The police are simply an extension of the prison Admin, engaging in lethal aggression and occupation over what has been proclaimed a "gang" by the prison system.

This "war" on Black people was so obvious to the judge in Shakur's suit that he was forced to notice that the Admin had "taken a race-based short cut and assumed that anything having to do with African-American culture could be banned under the guise of controlling the BGF."

The Witchhunt

This is more than mere censorship. The Admin actually theorizes Shakur's writing as a certain kind of act. The IGI guard says:

"The New Africans are those who have come to understand, even though they may have been born in the United States, they are descendants from one of many tribes of Africa. … Coupling the mindset of New Africans with the Revolutionary Nationalism or NARN forms the basis and beliefs of the BGF prison gang. In doing this, the teachings of NARN become more than just words; they become a belief in the concept and ideologies of NARN and the BGF."

The "theoretical" move here is the assertion that the "teachings" of NARN become "more than just words." [Blink] This expert prison gang investigator is saying that the teachings of NARN become beliefs in the concepts of NARN. That is, the thoughts of NARN become the thoughts of NARN.

And this tautology is then used as a means of understanding words as "more than just words." By raising tautology to the status of "activity," these words become actions against prison security. In short, power defines "threat" for itself by saying "these people are a security threat because they are a security threat."

We see this on the streets. When a cop shoots an unarmed person (usually of color), it is sufficient for him to say, "I felt threatened," to legitimize his act – despite videos demonstrating the opposite: Gary King was shot in the back walking away; Alan Blueford was shot while lying down, with his hands up; Michael Brown was shot a hundred feet from the cop. It is the Admin's words that become "more than just words."

In its own words, what the Admin claims is a threat are the ideas of autonomous Black identity (NARN and New Afrikan identity), an identity developed by Black people for themselves, rather than one concocted for them by white society, under cover of "law." Rooting out this identity is the field on which the Admin's witchhunt operates, much as medieval inquisitors sought to discover witches among the women of Europe.

Witchcraft Inquisitor: You women think that you can heal people using herbs. Only the devil thinks this, because it is outside the teachings of the church. Since you think this, you can only have gotten this thought from the devil. You are therefore in league with the devil and will be burned to death.

Prison Admin: You African Americans think you can reconstruct your identity through identification with Africa. Only subversives and security threats think this because it is outside the identity U.S. society intends for you. Since you think this, you can only have gotten this idea from a subversive organization, such as the BGF. You are therefore members of the BGF and will be destroyed in prison.

If the prosecution of gangs requires a witchhunt, then the threat they pose cannot be real. For a witchhunt, the concept of a threat becomes a cover for the logic of the witchhunt itself, which is to outlaw ideas and destroy the people who hold those ideas.

Its central purpose is to destroy Black and Brown identity on both a social and a cultural level, both inside and outside prison. The Admin's response to the identity it sees as a threat is to impose the "social death" that Orlando Patterson speaks of, in which being Black in the U.S. means being deprived of any identity other than that imposed by white power.

Today, this "social death" has become the real death of unceasing police murders of people of color on the streets. It has a wholly different character from street gang conflict.

Though these police shootings are designed to bring all Black and Brown people into submission, they have now had the opposite effect. They have brought about massive resistance, as we have seen since the murder of Michael Brown in Ferguson, demanding justice and the dismantling of police militarization, while fostering a now international recognition and insistence that "black lives matter," which has shown up in demonstrations in Europe and South America.

STEVE MARTINOT

The Black Guerrilla Family and Human Freedom

After Germany's defeat in World War II, the leadership of the Nazi Party was brought to trial in what has become known as the Nuremberg Process. From that process, new social principles emerged, concepts such as "genocide" and "crimes against humanity."

Naked and arbitrary aggression was outlawed, as was the concept of collective punishment (retaliation against a group for the act or existence of an individual). And to this it added as a social principle that every individual had the responsibility to refuse an illegal command – whether in the army, the police, an institutional administration or on the street.

In this article, the second in a series of three, I continue an examination of certain California prison Rules Violation Reports issued against a man in Pelican Bay named Abdul Olugbala Shakur. In the previous article, I argued that the prison administration's actions amount to a form of collective punishment.

Under the aegis of repressing a "gang" called the Black Guerrilla Family (BGF), the administration carried on a witchhunt against the political thinking of many Black prisoners and punished them by solitary confinement. Insofar as a witchhunt enforces the prohibition of ideas, the Nuremberg Principle requires all prison guards to refuse to enforce that prohibition.

The opposite occurs. This article will look at the notion of prison gang, its relation to the prisoner's need for defense and how that affects us beyond the prison wall.

On Shakur

As described previously, Shakur was charged with rules violations because of things he wrote in private letters to friends. In these letters, he speaks of the New Afrikan independence movement as a source of self-determined identity for African Americans and the role New Afrikan Revolutionary Nationalism (NARN) can play as part of ongoing resistance against anti-Black racism.

He also speaks of the George Jackson University (GJU), a school for learning Black and anti-colonialist history and resistance, of which he is a founder and open proponent. He proposes it as a means of establishing peace and unity between warring street gangs in the nation's Black communities.

Unbeknownst to many, Abdul Olugbala Shakur developed and wrote the original blueprint to the "Agreement to End Hostilities" in California Prisons that helped bring about the massive hunger strike of 2013, calling attention to denial of human rights in the prisons. And these write-ups charge and punish Shakur for advancing these thoughts.

Each report had the same form. A guard had read the letters, had written him up and then repeated certain "facts" about him – for instance, that he was a "validated" member of the BGF. The hearings then simply involved linking his thoughts to the BGF. Even when a letter quoted the warden's description of the BGF, it was considered "gang activity." As Shakur argued, this made him – and some 30 others in the Pelican Bay SHU – political prisoners.

The procedure is simple. The administration links certain ideas to an alleged group (which may or may not exist), outlaws the group as a "threat to prison security" and thus bans the ideas as constituting outlawed activity. Thus, it simply asserts that the GJU is a group for the "dissemination of BGF literature and training materials to communities and inmates." Where this literature is to be found remains unstated.

GJU brochures give long lists of works about Black resistance, African history and culture, and African American political organization. But there is no mention of BGF "literature." Nor does any appear on the internet (the many police oriented web pages that discuss the BGF) or in the UC Berkeley library catalogue.

Similarly, when Shakur refers to "us" in his letters, the administration adds parenthetically that this means "BGF members." Thus, he is denied his personhood.

The administration links certain ideas to an alleged group (which may or may not exist), outlaws the group as a "threat to prison security" and thus bans the ideas as constituting outlawed activity.

I know of a prisoner who had a book by George Jackson sent to him. It came from the publisher, it went through the mail room, the censors and inspectors, and was delivered to his cell. Months later, a different guard found the book in the person's cell, and wrote him up as a gang member, resulting in his being thrown in solitary.

Gangs in prison

There are gangs in the prisons, and they sometimes fight among themselves. That is true. "Gang" is defined by the state (CCR §3000, rule 3023a) as any group of three or more with a common name or identifying sign or symbols whose members have knowingly engaged in planning, organizing, threatening or financing or committing unlawful acts.

If any unlawful acts are attributed to Shakur, they are not mentioned in his write-ups. He is simply condemned to solitary for having been defined by the administration as a member of the BGF.

How is the BGF defined? The administration uses what is found on the web.

"The BGF was cofounded in 1966 by George Jackson. … The BGF is the most 'politically' oriented of the major prison gangs. It was formed as a Marxist-Maoist-Leninist revolutionary organization with specific goals to eradicate racism, struggle to maintain dignity in prison and overthrow the U.S. government. All members must be Black. Though small in number, the BGF has a very strict death oath which requires a life pledge of loyalty to the gang. Prospective members must be nominated by an existing member."

The idea that George Jackson founded the BGF is essential, though its factuality is denied by much police testimony in court. The story of Jackson's alleged "jailbreak" in 1971, as the reason for his murder in the San Quentin prison yard, is the original unlawful act for which the administration bans the BGF.

It is a fanciful story insofar as Jackson is said to have had one of two kinds of gun, that he had either shot his way into the Adjustment Center (solitary cell block) or shot his way out, was trying to break out by running toward the wall rather than the gate, and was the cause for five people having their throats slit inside the Adjustment Center with no prisoners getting any blood on themselves.

Many gangs are constructed along racial or ethnic lines. Fights between them are at times incited by guards to create an opportunity to shoot a few people and throw some more in solitary.

But all groups of prisoners need a means of self-defense against the administration to preserve personhood and social unity against the combination of racism, contempt and raw power. White prisoners sometimes get recognition for being white. At other prisons, they reaffirm their white personhood by attacking Black prisoners (in tacit alliance with the guards).

If the guards use "race" as an instrument of power against prisoners, white prisoners will use their social hierarchy (white over Black) to avoid being targeted. When the guards use hierarchy – their raw power – as an instrument against prisoners, white prisoners will use race and demand recognition in terms of white solidarity.

Thus, Black prisoners and other prisoners of color have to contend with both guards and white supremacist gangs, like the Aryan Brotherhood. Their need for self-defense is double.

Does the BGF exist?

The question arises about the BGF, does it actually exist? Or is it simply an instrument for the repression of Black people?

From what I have been told, the answer is that it exists. The real question is, in what form does it exist? As an organization, with meetings and by-laws? As the idea of an organization with which people can identify? Or as an identity of resistance to racial oppression? These are important distinctions. And in the outside world, an organization can be all three. But inside, that is more difficult.

For a ban to be legitimate, the administration would have to show the BGF was a real organization. To ban an idea is despotic and unconstitutional. And to ban an identity is cultural genocide.

For its political purposes, the administration seeks to erase these distinctions, banning ideas and identities in the name of banning an "organization." The power the administration gains by these means adds to the need for defensive organization on the part of the prisoners.

To "prove" an organization exists, there has to be some actual evidence, especially if one is going to condemn people through it. There must be membership lists and procedures by which actions were planned – reports of meetings, charters, rules, initiation rites, manifestos and leaflets, etc.

There was actually a constitution written, which the administration would confiscate. But that is not proof, since anyone can write one. It can even emerge from discussions and represent collective decisions made secretly somewhere in the yard. But something more would be needed if the group sought to attract members – which is what the administration's mention of "nomination" procedures implies.

Ultimately, the administration simply relies on its impunity, its power to define. To state the gang exists becomes proof of that existence. Membership is defined by upholding New Afrikan ideas – or reading George Jackson.

Jackson himself was clear on what he thought, and his strategy was simple. He understood the prison system to constitute concentration camps for Black people, as the Nazi camps did for Jews, and its purpose was to break and destroy all Black people in its clutches.

His own sentence was an atrocity – one-to-life for stealing $72. What galled him was (and I paraphrase) "that they never imagined that I would resist." His counsel to others is: "We must disabuse them of the idea that destroying us will be easy." And therein lies the BGF's "security threat." Only against a strategy of destruction does resistance become a threat.

The administration is also admitting that the BGF's dedication to eliminating racism is part of that threat. It thus admits that it needs anti-Black racism – and gains power from it.

Shakur is punished for legitimately (under the Nuremberg Principle) upholding the idea of resistance to anti-Black racism. When an idea is criminalized by a power structure to oppress people, a crime is being committed by that power structure. In that sense, the BGF has greater legitimacy under international law than the prison administration itself.

The BGF exists, but not as the administration says it does. The real absence of proof means it exists as a source of identity, an identification with the ideas of anti-racism and human rights.

In focusing on loyalty to the BGF, the administration raises another issue, that of allegiance, which becomes another aspect of threat. If a gang's purpose is collective defense, then allegiance will not produce disruptive violence, since it is defensive.

Allegiance is a threat because the prison system needs allegiance to itself and not to other organizations. Its own structural criminality – composed of kidnapping, torture, violation of human rights, violation of civil rights, beatings, assault, denial of due process, etc. – can be legitimized only through general acceptance of those crimes as legitimate.

Only allegiance to the idea of self-decriminalization will valorize those acts. Thus, any alternate allegiance will disrupt this self-decriminalization. In particular, every guard must give allegiance to the prison system since they are involved in the commission of torture as well.

On the other hand, prisoner self-defense does not require "allegiance" but rather solidarity. Solidarity says, "We stand shoulder to shoulder" and if anything happens, "I have your back." Allegiance is based on the idea that "I am watching you to insure that you live up to the loyalty that I expect from you." Solidarity produces an identity of resistance. Loyalty (as allegiance) marks hierarchy and a need for justification.

The difference between allegiance and solidarity is evident in the censorship of the prisoners.

The Meaning of Censorship

Censorship criminalizes ideas because it punishes those who propound those ideas, such as it punishes Shakur by extending solitary for speaking of NARN or Black August, for instance.

But it has an insidious character; Shakur is accused of "promoting gang activity" when he suggests that the George Jackson University can bring unity and peace among the street gangs of the Black communities because he is "attempting to utilize the NARN concepts to indoctrinate the street gangs."

The officer testifies that Shakur is aware that promoting the BGF indoctrinates gang activity – though Shakur states that it is constitutionally protected political thought. "Gang activity" thus attaches to the stating of certain ideas. As the officer says, in "coupling the mindset of New Africans with the revolutionary nationalism of NARN, ... the teachings of NARN become more than just words."

But what do they become? Directives? Programming? For the administration, "teachings" indoctrinate. To "teach" is to determine what others will do and think. The implication is that when people hear these ideas, they automatically become active believers, led willy-nilly into gang activity. Censorship criminalizes ideas because it punishes those who propound those ideas, such as it punishes Shakur by extending solitary for speaking of NARN or Black August, for instance.

By simply bringing the ideas of the GJU to street gang attention, they will be indoctrinated – which must be prevented. For the administration, such readers or listeners are incapable of thinking for themselves. They will be controlled by what they read or hear.

Thus, the administration's censorship violates the freedom of the reader. The reader cannot be permitted to read what the writer wrote. All readers are both deprived of their freedom and dehumanized at the same time. That means us.

Where the prison administration speaks for Shakur – and criminalizes him in order to decriminalize itself – it also speaks for the reader and criminalizes the reader in advance. Where the prison administration extends the prison to imprisonment inside the prison, it also extends the prison to all people outside it, by violating their freedom as readers.

Let's look at this carefully. To read a text, one must interpret its words, first their dictionary meaning and then the meaning they bestow upon phrases and sentences. Grammatical structure, as the context for words, changes their meanings and requires interpretation. Finally, one must interpret the flow of sentences to see what the text is doing.

One engages at least three levels of interpretation in order to read something. And one must do this freely.

Whatever the author had in mind, the reader's freedom to interpret signifies that what the reader finds in the text is determined by the act of reading, not the act of writing. Different people read the same piece of writing differently.

In this sense, it is not sensible to say that a piece of writing is "inflammatory," for instance. The act of being "enflamed" belongs to the reader, not the writer. To make a rule or law against inflammatory writing is nonsense. To permit writing to be disseminated only if it is non-inflammatory is despotic. It denies the reader the freedom to be a person.

And similarly for the notion of "indoctrination." Writing cannot "indoctrinate" because the reader must be free to read interpretively. Only violence can indoctrinate a person.

The freedom of the writer is guaranteed by the First Amendment as freedom of speech. The freedom of the reader is also guaranteed as the freedom of the press. Though suppression or control of the press can enforce ignorance, the press cannot indoctrinate.

As essential to its self-decriminalization, the prison administration must extend the paradigm of imprisonment far beyond its own walls and destroy alternative ideas. Censorship suppresses the freedom of the reader in order to create a social population that will only read what the administration gives them to read. It is thus an attempt to control the rest of us. It is thus a dehumanization of us all.

To censor an author as a threat is to engage in the collective punishment of people unknown and unidentifiable by curtailing their freedom in the name of punishing the author. It is to blame the author for what the reader thinks.

Note on pornography: There is a similar issue around pornography. Visual pornography, films, pictures and theatrical performances constitute an objectification of sex and sexuality by removing it from the realm of sensuality and shifting it to that of spectacle, an objective interaction between things – things that happen to be body parts.

But it also depends on an objectification of women. In a patriarchal society such as the U.S., male hegemony is already an objectification of women. It establishes a subject-object relation for which men are the subject. What a man does as a person he does as an individual.

As generalized objects – and generalization is a form of violence – women are "mass produced." Men can walk away from the objectification imposed on them by their performance in pornography. What a woman does as an object is something that happens to her, and thus happens to all women. She cannot walk away from her objectification in visual pornography.

But for literature, the situation is different, because it is written. The reader has to interpret what is written. The film image is not symbolic, but presentational.

STEVE MARTINOT

The Criminality of Solitary Confinement

Introduction

In this series of articles, we have traced the various mechanisms whereby the prison procedures of "gang validation" are used to deny the civil rights, the human rights and even the humanity of the prisoners. These procedures mark the criminality of the prison administration, the California Department of Corrections.

We have been considering the case of Abdul Olugbala Shakur, who has been in solitary confinement for decades. In the past, the administration had broken Shakur's contact with his mother, his spiritual father and others. In its more recent attacks, it has charged him with "gang activity" for having written about certain matters in private letters to friends and compatriots.

In the various Rules Violation Reports on these charges, the administration has revealed its own criminality. In particular, it has engineered witchhunts in the name of gang control and despotically imposed extensive censorship on prisoners' reading material and correspondence.

These engineered campaigns constitute aggression not only against prisoners but against all of us as well, insofar as we are barred from their information about their situation. In addition, the impunity of this criminal aggressiveness against the political thinking of prisoners demonstrates, more than anything, the necessity for political resistance by the prisoners themselves, for their psychological survival, which then gets called "gang activity."

What many Black prisoners have adopted, in order to defend themselves against the administration, is an identification with the ideas of New Afrikan Nationalism, as a self-chosen identity. As self-chosen, it offers opposition, alternative and resistance against the identity traditionally imposed upon Black people by a discriminatory society.

In Shakur's case, he is prosecuted for mentioning New Afrika, New Afrikan Revolutionary Nationalism, Black August, George Jackson and the George Jackson University in private letters to friends – and given more time in solitary. It is to "outlaw" these ideas as well as identification with them that the administration has associated them with "gang activity."

Imprisonment is an act of violence designed to separate a person from society. The rationale of "protecting" society against violent people fails in view of the fact that 70 percent of all prisoners are there for victimless crimes.

Censorship is designed to further isolate prisoners from society. But this patently contradicts the pretended "legitimate" purpose of prison, namely, to return a criminal to society as a better law-abiding person. To return to society, one must have maintained a relation to it. Insofar as censorship breaks that relation, it makes reentry difficult.

But we already know that the legislated obstructions placed in the way of former prisoners – barring access to social services, public housing and most employment – makes reentry practically impossible, essentially guaranteeing recidivism. "Reentry" becomes a fraudulent term whose real meaning is social exile.

Why would recidivism be built into the system? So that the administration can say that certain people, mostly people of color, are incorrigible and must be permanently removed from society. The real point of imprisonment, then, is not to establish respect for law and decency but to implement segregation.

It is not to correct bad behavior but to destroy people and communities. It signifies that "crime" is not the problem the judicial machine is constructed to resolve but rather the existence of Black and Brown people.

Prison is today, for the most part, a project to rebuild the segregationism torn down by the Civil Rights Movement. Today, 75 percent of all prisoners are people of color.

We see this fact unfold in its extreme in the murder of Black and Brown people by the police in the streets. In 2012, over 600 unarmed people of color were killed by the police. In 2014, that figure rose to over 1,020 (the freethoughtproject.com). In 2014, as well, in the prisons of Florida alone, over 340 people were killed by the guards (Daily Kos, 1/14/15).

The Criminality of Extended Isolation

Shakur had been in isolation for decades, along with 80,000 other prisoners in the U.S. It was to protest this fact that prisoners organized a hunger strike in July 2013. Its demands were simply for "human rights, decent food, correspondence" with the outside, fairness in administration treatment and an end to indefinite solitary confinement. Since that hunger strike, Shakur has been attacked and harassed by the administration, using their rules violation procedures to do so (as outlined in the previous articles, "Prisons, Gangs, Witchhunts and White Supremacy" and "The Black Guerrilla Family and Human Freedom").

Shakur has described the reality of isolation in an essay ("What is Solitary Confinement?" previously published in the Bay View 10/18/14). To place a person in a small cell with a steel door and no personal contact with others is only the technical instrumentality of isolation.

According to the U.N., and recognized in the U.S., such isolation is sufficient to drive a person mad. It is a mode of torture whose purpose is the destruction of personhood.

But there are always other prisoners in an isolation cellblock. They can speak to each other through doors and corridors and hear the others' screams. So the administration, as Shakur describes it, creates social, political and psychological isolation by engineering who the others in the cellblock will be.

To place a Black prisoner, for instance, adjacent to someone who aggressively hates Black people will be to subject him to a ceaselessly hostile and aggressive environment. Thus, the many hatreds inculcated in U.S. society – ethnic, racial, gender, ideological, demographic etc. – are used by the administration to assist in the further destruction of intellect and personhood.

That destruction is not permitted to any institution in this country by any law or ethic, which means that it is itself totally criminal behavior by the prison institution. What astounds is that the prison industry schemes about how to torture each prisoner with these extreme forms of institutional sadism.

Though the term "sadism" is a psychological term that refers to individual psychology, what the prison industry is proving is that these psychological terms can also refer to institutions. The fraud that disguises these procedures of torture politically lies in calling them "control" procedures, thus making them seem necessary, as if prison were not already absolute control.

The Impossibility of Justice Amid Punishment for Thought
With respect to the rules violation write-ups by which people are kept in solitary, their purpose is punishment for thought. As indicated above, associating certain thoughts with gang activity gives the administration the power to ban those thoughts in the name of outlawing gangs. Though it rationalizes this as defense against anti-social disruption, it is the administration that defines gangs, and thus

defines disruption. The real purpose remains to charge and convict people for what they think.

We know how distant that is from law enforcement. Law enforcement means that, in the event a crime is committed, a person suspected of committing that crime is brought to trial to be decided by a jury of his/her peers.

In the U.S., this is what passes for "justice." To be a real system of justice, there would have to be checks and balances against the ability of the police or prosecutors to frame a person for something they didn't do. That doesn't exist.

When George Ryan was governor of Illinois, he found out that one out of every six persons on death row was innocent of the crime for which he was to be executed – framed by the judicial system – and in 2003 ended the death penalty. Of course, the revenge ethic that is fulfilled by imprisonment already makes justice impossible because it doubles the criminality and violence in society simply through the violence and criminality of its vengeance. It also provides a role model for further social violence.

But beyond that, there are a number of corruptions of the "law enforcement" paradigm: 1) A person can be convicted because suspected of having committed some as yet unknown crime. 2) A person can be convicted for having thought about committing a specific crime. 3) A person can be convicted for having thought about committing some as yet unknown crime. 4) A person can be convicted of having thoughts that do not constitute crimes or criminality but simply for having such thoughts. 5) And finally, a person can be convicted for being suspected of having certain unspecified thoughts, which nevertheless are suspected to constitute crimes, simply because suspected.

The first occurs with racial profiling, in which the police commit an act of suspicion, and hold a person while they look for a crime the person might possibly have committed, depriving them of liberty while they do so. The second occurs every time someone is charged under a conspiracy statute, which means that the person, in conversation with others, thought about committing a crime. If the crime is actually committed, then the existence of that conversation can be considered pre-meditation, but then it is no longer "conspiracy."

The third occurs when an officer shoots someone for disobeying a command and states that he, the officer, felt threatened by the suspect. In such a case, the officer is charging the suspect with felonious assault and then prosecuting, convicting and punishing the person by shooting him.

The fourth occurs when a police officer shoots someone who disobeys an officer's command, for instance, by running away, thus assuming the criminality of the person's thoughts and convicting by punishing him in the moment – as Officer Gonzales did when he shot Gary King in the back as King walked away in Oakland in 2007. The list of people to whom this has happened is longer than the list of people on death row in California.

The fifth occurs when a person is killed by the police for simply refusing to be handcuffed or refusing to open the door to the police. We can mention Kayla Moore, Eric Garner, Kenneth Chamberlain, Ramarley Graham … but again, the list is very long.

When an officer shoots and kills a person, as Officer Wilson shot Michael Brown as he stood 100 feet away with his hands up, and is exonerated of any wrongdoing, the state, in so exonerating him, is saying that the officer acted according to state policy. In other words, in acting as prosecutor, judge and jury, the officer has properly performed as an extension of the state's judicial machinery.

The revenge ethic that is fulfilled by imprisonment already makes justice impossible because it doubles the criminality and violence in society simply through the violence and criminality of its vengeance. It also provides a role model for further social violence.

Only when involved in actual law enforcement are police officers not extensions of the judicial process. Then they are acting as actual police officers, policing the society according to the law. But in the other instances, the police have taken on state functions that are not given to them.

The witchhunting process by which prisoners are brought up on rules violation charges in California prisons, and thrown in solitary or kept in solitary for what they think or read, constitutes a conjunction of all these travesties of justice. The person in prison whose thoughts are defined by the administration as "evidence" of gang activity is not only suspected of criminality, but suspected of conspiring, of rule violations, of thinking about rule violations and of thinking about disobeying the rules in order to disobey in all these respects. Gang validation amounts to conviction on all counts.

The real travesty is that the prison administration pretends it is engaged in legitimate judicial process. In its hearing reports, there are sections labeled "due process," "investigation," "witnesses," "plea" and "testimony" as if they were real.

Ironically, in every one of Shakur's write-ups, the hearing officer denied Shakur permission to have a witness, declaring that what the witness would say would be irrelevant to the case. This not only cancelled the witness's existence as a person, but it deprived the prisoner of a defense, as well as due process. The judge, in speaking for someone who isn't there, thus ceases to be a judge, and becomes a despot.

Isolation is for the Purpose of Driving People Mad

It is known that isolation will drive people mad. Like all torture, it is destructive and is understood to be so in law and in U.N. proclamation. Yet entire prison systems (Pelican Bay, Marion, Lexington, etc.) are based upon facilitating solitary confinement. They are institutions built on the principle of destroying human beings.

The administration claims that isolation is necessary to punish people who are violent or who break prison rules. But these prisons were built first, before they had people to punish in this way. They were built with the knowledge that their operation would destroy people. Afterwards, strategies and policies were developed for filling them. The notion of gang validation is one of those strategies.

The purpose of torturing people is to destroy what they think without damaging the person physically – and without committing murder. The administration can say it is defending society against violence rather than committing it. But this simply dovetails with the rhetoric of "correction" (The Department of Correction), whose reality is to intentionally guarantee recidivism.

The False Purpose of Imprisonment

In light of this project which the prison system fulfills in the U.S., it is utmost blindness to uphold the idea that prisons have a role to play in dealing with people who assault others and who rape and murder them. We hear it all the time: "People have to take responsibility for what they have done to others. We have to get them off the street."

This is empty if it does not also mean doing so to the perpetrators of institutional criminality – the guards and prison administration, the cops who shoot or beat people on the street, as well as those who legislatively legitimize – through inactivity – or even authorize the torture of solitary confinement. They all need to be held responsible for the violence they impose on society.

Unfortunately, none of this responds to the real issue of justice. It doesn't even ask if imprisonment itself is unjust or not. In its silence on that issue, the call for imprisonment affirms that the question of justice is irrelevant.

Indeed, the very desperation contained in that question – "What are we going to do about violent people?" – names the injustice of imprisonment and of its administration. Instead, mass incarceration and solitary confinement are given legal rationalization, though they are forms of psychological destruction, in order that civil society can think that everything is OK and that justice is served.

There are two dimensions to the social acceptance of imprisonment. The first is tradition. Prison is the way Western society has always dealt with those who break the law. The second is violence, reflecting a desire to torture people. Removal from society inflicts pain, as does confinement to a cage.

If we are serious about halting anti-social transgressions – for which persons are ostensibly to be held responsible – then we have to find an alternative because imprisonment is by nature anti-social and transgressive, against persons, families and communities.

If we are serious about justice, then we have to recognize that the injustice of solitary confinement reveals a fundamental desire for injustice at the core of the culture of the U.S. It marks the real desire to deprive people of human rights – outside on the street as well as inside the prison.

Pain, suffering and psychological destruction are the intentions society manifests through imprisonment. It is true that it makes some people feel good about themselves and that the violence committed constitutes a mark of virtue for them.

But for that very reason, as the implementation of a revenge ethic, prisons and imprisonment have no socially redeeming value. They are wholly corrupting, even of those people who support them as an institution.

For those of us who believe in justice and democracy, the real crime problem in the U.S. is the prison system itself and its judicial machine. Together they are making justice and democracy practically impossible.

CONCLUSION

ABDUL OLUGBALA SKAIUR

CONCLUSION

Concrete Scholars in its cumulative acquisition can serve to be an indictment of a society that has lost its sense of humanity. Our books contain both the qualitative and quantitative property to validate for all practical purposes the inhumanities of a society that hallucinates of moral grandeur of a self-proclamation of its alleged humanity. In executing this indictment we make no claims of perfection, but sitting in solitary confinement for decades allowed us to deeply explore the depths of the anatomy of this society, and along with this diagnostic paradigm we confirm the symptoms of an aligning society. e. g. 1) Institutionalized Racism 2) Institutionalized Sexism 3) Racial Based Oppression. 4) A Deliberate Imposition of Poverty 5) Imperialism 6) An Inherent Greed/Materialism, just to name a few.

Our book provides a comprehensive indictment to serve as a medium to facilitate, if not expedite ones capacity to understand the anatomy of an immoral society trapped within its own inhumanities under a false cloak of a self-pronouncement of humanity's protector.

—Abdul Olugbala Shakur
Concrete Scholars
George Jackson University (GJU)

Abdul Olugbala Shakur
James Harvey
C-4884/B-2-128
P.O. Box 5102
Delano, CA 93216
Kern Valley State Prison

Joka Heshima Jinsai
Heshima Denham
J-38283/B-2-117
P.O. Box 5102
Delano, CA 93216
Kern Valley State Prison

Notes

INTRODUCTION
Joka Heshima Jinsai
Concrete Scholars
[1]Gómez, Alan Eladio. "Resisting Living Death at Marion Federal Penitentiary, 1972." New York: MARHO: The Radical Historians' Organization, Inc., 1996. doi 10.1215/01636545-2006-004; Issue 96
[2]"Convention against Torture and Other Cruel, Inhuman or Degrading Treatment or Punishment," December 10, 1984. https://www.ohchr.org/en/professionalinterest/pages/cat.aspx.

CHAPTER THREE
"The Antithesis of Oppression: How I survived 20 Years of Solitary Confinement"
Joka Heshima Jinsai
[1]George Jackson University
Jackson, George L. "Blood in My Eye." Essay. In *Blood in My Eye*, 2–87. Baltimore: Black Classic Press, 1990.
[2]Gómez, Alan Eladio. "Resisting Living Death at Marion Federal Penitentiary, 1972." New York: MARHO: The Radical Historians' Organization, Inc., 1996. doi 10.1215/01636545-2006-004; Issue 96
[3]Committee on the Judiciary. "Marion Penitentiary - 1985: Oversight Hearing before the Subcommittee on Courts, Civil Liberties, and the Administration of Justice of the Committee on the Judiciary House of Representatives." Riverside. Accessed November 15, 2019. https://books.google.com.
[4]Griffin, Eddie. "Breaking Men's Minds: Behavior Control and Human Experimentation at the Federal Prison in Marion, Illinois." Journal of Prisoners on Prisons, vol. 4, no. 2, 1993, pp. 16–28.

[5]McLeod, S. A. (2015, Jan 14) Psychological theories of depression. . Simply Psychology. https://www.simplypsychology.org/depression.html

CHAPTER FIVE
Chess vs Checkers
Abdul Olugbala Shakur
[1]Valentine, Joe A. "Review Board Suggests Pelican Bay Prisoner Stop Political Writing for Favorable Placement." San Francisco Bay View National Black Newspaper . May 13, 2014. https://sfbayview.com/2014/05/review-board-suggests-pelican-bay-prisoner-stop- political-writing-for-favorable-placement/.

CHAPTER EIGHT
"A Day in the Life of an Imprisoned Revolutionary"
Joka Heshima Jinsai
[1]Camp, Jordan T. "The Sound before the Fury." Chapter. In Incarcerating the Crisis: Freedom Struggles and the Rise of the Neoliberal State, 89–89. Oakland, CA: University of California Press, 2016.
[2]Committee on the Judiciary. "Marion Penitentiary - 1985: Oversight Hearing before the Subcommittee on Courts, Civil Liberties, and the Administration of Justice of the Committee on the Judiciary House of Representatives." Riverside. Accessed November 15, 2019. https://books.google.com.
[3]Kamrava, Mehran. "From Rebellion to Revolution." Chapter. In A Concise History of Revolution, 40–40. New York, NY: Cambridge University Press, 2019.
[4]Alinsky, Saul. "Communication." Chapter. In Rules for Radicals, 85–85. New York, NY: Random House, 1989.

CHAPTER NINE
"Amend the 13th: Abolish Legal Slavery in Amerika Movement
    Mission Statement"
Joka Heshima Jinsai, Founder
    [1]Dayan, Colin. "Civil Death." Chapter. In The Law Is a
        White Dog: How Legal Rituals Make and Unmake
        Persons, 61–65. Princeton, NJ: Princeton
        University Press, 2013.

CHAPTER TEN
"On Self-Defense Against Racist Murder: A Discussion on the
    Culture of Hate and Violence in US
Society and the Rationality of Securing New Afrikan Communities"
Joka Heshima Jinsai
    [1]Fall, Bernard B. "Ho Chi Minh on Revolution: Selected
        Writings 1920-66." New York: New American
        Library, Inc., February 1968.
    [2]Greene, Robert. "Create a Threatening Pretense:
        Deterrence Strategies." Essay. In The 33 Strategies
        of War, 123–36. New York: Penguin Books, 2008.
    [3]Sayles, James Yaki. "Meditations on Franz Fanon's
        Wretched of the Earth: New Afrikan
        Revolutionary Writings." Chicago: Spear & Shield
        Publications, 2010.
    [4]DuBois, William Edward Burghardt. "Darkwater: Voices
        from Within the Veil." New York: Dover
        Publications, 1999.
    [5]Reich, Wilhelm. "The Race Theory." Chapter. In The
        Mass Psychology of Fascism: (3. Print.), 80–80.
        New York: Farrar, Straus, & Giroux, 1970.
    [6]Johnson, Kevin, Megan Hoyer, and Brad Heath. "Local
        Police Involved in 400 Killings per Year."
        Washington, August 14, 2014.
        https://www.usatoday.com/story/news/nation/2
        014/08/14/police-killings-data/14060357/.
    [7]Sayles, James Yaki. "Meditations on Franz Fanon's
        Wretched of the Earth: New Afrikan

Revolutionary Writings." Chicago: Spear & Shield
        Publications, 2010.
[8]Greene, Robert, and Robert Greene. "Create a
        Threatening Presence: Deterrence Strategies."
        Chapter. In The 33 Strategies of War: Concise
        Edition, 124–36. London: Profile, 2008.
[9]Gramlich, John, and Katherine Schaeffer. "7 Facts about
        Guns in the U.S." Pew Research Center. Pew
        Research Center, October 22, 2019.
        https://www.pewresearch.org/fact-
        tank/2019/10/22/facts-about-guns-in-united-
        states/.

CHAPTER ELEVEN
"Trayvon, Christian, Jason, Gerardo, Kendrec and Nine Children
        in Afghanistan: A Discussion
of Race, Violence and the Authoritarian Psychology."
Joka Heshima Jinsai

[1]Sayles, James Yaki. "Meditations on Franz Fanon's
        Wretched of the Earth: New Afrikan
        Revolutionary Writings." Chicago: Spear & Shield
        Publications, 2010.
[2]Cornel West, "The Ignoble Parody of Modernity," in The
        Cornel West Reader, First (New York, NY: Basic
        Civitas Books, 1999), p. 52.
[3]"Internet Archive." Full text of "Mass Psychology of
        Fascism - Wilhelm Reich. American Library
        Association. Accessed December 19, 2019.
        https://archive.org/stream/MassPsychologyOfFa
        scism-WilhelmReich/mass-psychology-
        reich_djvu.txt.
[4]Serwer, Adam. "Private Prisons Spend Millions Pushing
        Bad Policy." The American Prospect. The
        American Prospect, Inc., June 27, 2011.
        https://prospect.org/article/private-prisons-
        spend-millions-pushing-bad-policy/.

5Jackson, George L. "On Withdrawl." Chapter. In Blood in My Eye, 117–26. New York: Random House, 1972.
6Genet, Jean. "Soledad Brother: The Prison Letters of George Jackson." RBG Street Scholars Think Tank, July 2010.

Abdul Olugbala Shakur

Long Live the Graceful Guerrillas

Joka Heshima Jinsai